Safe Dieting for Teens

The Facts You Need to Know to Choose the Diet You Want

Fact: Structured diets that completely change your eating patterns are doomed to fail.

Fact: The only diet plan that will work long term is one you can live with for the rest of your life.

Fact: Small changes make a huge difference. Cut out one soda a day and lose twenty-four pounds in a year.

Fact: Weight loss is just math – fewer calories + more movement.

Fact: It's much harder for girls and women to lose weight than it is for boys and men.

Fact: You can lose weight while still eating fast foods.

Fact: Choices have consequences. Learn how to make wise ones.

LINDA OJEDA, PhD, is an author and speaker on nutrition, health, and weight loss. In this book she outlines a flexible diet plan and provides the nutritional information needed for designing a safe and effective weight-loss program. She also offers something more: an overall approach to improving self-esteem and general health.

*To my children,
Jill and Joey,
who are no longer teens*

Ordering
Trade bookstores in the U.S. and Canada please contact:

Publishers Group West
1700 Fourth Street, Berkeley CA 94710
Phone: (800) 788-3123   Fax: (510) 528-3444

Hunter House books are available at bulk discounts for textbook course adoptions; to qualifying community, health-care, and government organizations; and for special promotions and fund-raising.
For details please contact:

Special Sales Department
Hunter House Inc., PO Box 2914, Alameda CA 94501-0914
Phone: (510) 865-5282   Fax: (510) 865-4295
E-mail: ordering@hunterhouse.com

Individuals can order our books from most bookstores,
by calling **(800) 266-5592**, or from our website at
www.hunterhouse.com

Safe Dieting for Teens

SECOND EDITION

Linda Ojeda, PhD

Hunter House
PUBLISHERS

Hunter House Inc., Publishers
PO Box 2914
Alameda CA 94501-0914

Library of Congress Cataloging-in-Publication Data

Ojeda, Linda.
Safe dieting for teens / Linda Ojeda. – 2nd ed.
p. cm.
Includes bibliographical references and index.
ISBN-13: 978-0-89793-502-9 (pbk.)
ISBN-10: 0-89793-502-0 (pbk.)
1. Obesity in adolescence–Prevention.   2. Reducing diets.
3. Teenagers–Nutrition.   I. Title.
RJ399.C6O38 2007
613.2'50835–dc22   2007025188

Project Credits

Cover Design: Brian Dittmar Graphic Design	Publicity Assistant: Alexi Ueltzen
	Rights Coordinator: Candace
Book Production: John McKercher	Groskreutz
Copy Editor: Kelley Blewster	Customer Service Manager:
Proofreader: John David Marion	Christina Sverdrup
Indexer: Nancy D. Peterson	Order Fulfillment: Washul Lakdhon
Acquisitions Editor: Jeanne Brondino	Administrator: Theresa Nelson
Editor: Alexandra Mummery	Computer Support: Peter
Senior Marketing Associate:	Eichelberger
Reina Santana	Publisher: Kiran S. Rana

Printed and Bound by Bang Printing, Brainerd, Minnesota

Manufactured in the United States of America

9 8 7 6 5 4 3 2 1   Second Edition   08 09 10 11 12

Contents

Important Note

Introduction

This was a difficult book to write. I have mixed emotions about helping you lose weight if that is your issue. My heart goes out to all of you who are overweight. I want to help you drop those unwanted pounds safely and with as little difficulty as possible while also encouraging you to eat healthily and achieve a level of fitness that is right for you. On the other hand, I don't want you to think that you are not okay if you don't lose weight. I don't want you to believe that who you are depends on how much weight you carry. You are so much more than your dress size or pants size. So that's my dilemma. I'm torn between wanting to help you, because I know I can, and wanting you to see yourself as someone who is important and unique, with special talents and abilities, even if you aren't currently at your ideal weight.

I wrote this book over ten years ago because it was obvious that teens were inching up in weight and many of them were resorting to unhealthy practices to take the weight off. I saw them skip meals, take laxatives, drink "magic" potions, experiment with fad diets, exercise excessively, vomit after eating, and even starve themselves, sometimes to death. I thought I could help by telling them that these "quick but not-so-easy" solutions do not work. In fact they are often the things that make it more difficult to lose weight the next time around. But guess what? The health educators, doctors, and even the media didn't trust *you* to take control of your own health. It was the thinking at the time that if you were encouraged to diet, you would become anorexic or be drawn to other severe eating disorders. And I must admit that for some of you this was true, but not for the majority of teens who just wanted to tackle their extra pounds. Not every teen (or pre- or post-teen) who wants to lose weight turns to drastic measures. However, in case you are at risk for taking dieting to the extreme, I will alert you to some obvious signs.

Let me tell you a little about why I am qualified to give you advice. I'm a certified nutritionist by education, and I have many years of experience working for some of the leading weight-loss companies, from a medically supervised fasting program to one that provides ready-made meals. I've worked individually with doctors to help people figure out a program that works for them. And I, too, have struggled with weight issues since I was a sophomore in high school. Believe me, I have tried many diets myself. I've pored over the scientific research to find out what works, and I've watched women, men, teens, and children of all ages lose, gain, lose, and gain hundreds of the same pounds over and over.

In my years of research and observation, I have learned an important truth. **Fad diets do not work forever.** Sure, you may lose pounds quickly, and you may even keep them off for a while, but trust me on this: **95 percent of people on diets regain their weight.** You want to know why? Most diets are a short-term fix for a long-term problem. They deprive you of foods you like, and they set up a physical and emotional condition in your body that makes you hungry, not to mention a little crazy. When you give in to the urge to eat, you feel frustrated that you don't have willpower, and you become convinced that you are and always will be a failure. These strict diets also make it more difficult to lose weight the next time you try to do so, because your body rebels against a lack of adequate nutrition by stubbornly holding on to your stored fat. It is my hope to save you the time, money, and heartbreak of this repeated cycle that we older dieters have experienced too many times.

Many years ago, I worked individually with dieters who failed on various programs to help them figure out why they regained their weight. At first, I couldn't understand how this happened, especially since most of those who came back time after time were such perfect dieters. While they were on the program, they didn't even let themselves *smell* anything they weren't supposed to eat. Strangely, I noticed that the people who "cheated" by adding a vegetable, or sneaking an apple or a cookie, seemed to be more successful. It soon became obvious to me. The perfect dieters could not make the transition from the "diet program" to real life. They were either "on" the diet or "off" the diet. And the successful cheaters found ways to make changes they could live with. It wasn't an all-or-nothing plan for them. The moral to this story is **the closer the "weight-loss" diet is to a real, everyday, livable eating plan, the easier it is to follow and maintain.** And the best part is "no guilt." Eventually, you have to arrive at a life plan, one that you can live with day after day. So why not just start there rather than being "on" or "off" a diet that is doomed for failure?

I have found that weight loss can be achieved and maintained if the food options are designed around what the person likes, *and* if the plan fits in with their habits, social life, and school or work schedule. I'm sure this is why teens were especially unsuccessful in structured programs. It set them apart from their peers. Made them seem different. They couldn't go out for pizza with friends or grab a hamburger after the movies, so they stayed home and felt left out. Giving up your social life or feeling like you're weird is not a good trade-off for losing weight.

The latest research on dieting shows that many of the common weight-loss attempts fail desperately. Fad diets, ultra-low-fat diets, high-protein/low-carb diets, skipping meals, and swallowing diet pills do not work. What does succeed is a plan that is based on *lowering calories* and *increasing activity*. It's not a difficult concept, but it's one you need to figure out for yourself. With a little advice and encouragement from me, you are actually going to design your own diet plan that includes foods you like to eat – ones you can order at a restaurant, buy at the grocery store, or prepare easily at home. I'm not going to ask you to count calories, fat grams, or carbohydrates. I find that it's not necessary, and fixating too much on food can potentially lead to obsessive behavior in some people. **Eating should be a pleasure, not a punishment.**

I know that many of you hang out at fast-food establishments several times a week. You don't have to avoid these places when you're on a diet because there are foods you can order and still lose weight. You may not be aware that some of the popular fast-food meals contain an entire day's worth of calories. Fortunately, that's not all they have to offer. You can actually get something that will work into your plan. Granted, there are times when you may want a Big Mac or a large fries. That's your choice. But at least you will know that you have options and you can select how you want to spend your calories.

So, this is not a typical diet, but you will drop pounds. I will not tell you specifically what to eat, and I will not plan your daily menus. I will not provide a list of "good" foods and "bad" foods. Nothing is off limits. I don't believe that we should categorize foods as ones we can eat (carrots and cottage cheese) and ones we can't (doughnuts and ice cream). I don't have to tell you what happens when we're told we *can't* have something! The forbidden food just keeps calling our name until the last crumb has been devoured. I also don't like connecting guilty feelings to one of my favorite pastimes. It takes away the pleasure of eating, and that's a shame. Eating is fun; we should enjoy the experience. So if you're craving a chocolate doughnut, go for it. Eat it slowly, and enjoy every morsel. After all, tomorrow is another day.

By now, are you thinking that you picked up the wrong book? Yes, this book is about losing weight. But it's not about denial. It's about *choices*. **Losing weight is not a mystery; it's math.** You have to lower your caloric intake, burn calories through exercise, or both. Those are the options. However, there are many ways to accomplish this goal, and you can decide which way works best for you. For example, you can cut down on the amount of food you eat, you can substitute foods that have less fat or sugar in them, you can space your meals, and you can figure out how you want to burn more calories. The secret is, *you* decide what route to take (not me), because what *you* choose, you will follow. This is *your* diet. You design it based on the information in this book and your own personal research. And when you succeed, it's because of you, not me.

Since making good choices is the key to success, you need to know exactly what you are doing right now in terms of *what* you eat, *when* you eat, and *why* you eat. **Certain lifestyle practices make weight loss**

easier; others make it harder. Some habits are a breeze to change; others are nearly impossible. Once this is understood, you can start making realistic plans to change some of your behaviors. Don't worry. You won't have to totally change your life. And, you can take it slowly. Get used to making one change at a time. Believe me, this is the easiest, most effective way to get rid of your extra pounds.

I do not promise that you will be slim and trim by the end of the month or even by summer. What I do guarantee is that if you hang in there and follow the principals, you will lose your weight safely and you will also keep it off.

I know you're anxious, and I know that the diets that promise you can lose ten pounds in a week are enticing, but remember, *they don't work*. Please be patient. It didn't take you two months to put the weight on, and it won't take a few weeks to take it off. As you start this program, think about it as something you are staying with for a while. Think of it as learning a new skill, like playing tennis or the guitar. Once you've been taught the fundamentals, all you have to do is practice. At first it seems awkward and difficult, but after a while it comes easily. Controlling your weight won't always be the struggle it is today. Honest.

How to Use This Book

Don't rush to start immediately. Get used to the idea that this is what you want for your health and for yourself. Read through the book, highlighting things that jump out from the page and speak to you. Write in it, not just in the obvious spaces I've provided, but in the margins whenever something resonates with you or triggers your own thoughts and ideas. This is *your* project. It's not shock therapy, like other programs. It will take time, but you will gain the tools you need to make better choices, about —

✗ selecting foods to support weight loss

✗ knowing when to eat

✗ finding out why you overeat

✗ spotting unhealthy diet schemes

✗ selecting your own exercise program

✗ adding healthy foods to your life

✗ feeling good about yourself all the time

You are going to ease into losing weight by making small changes that will eventually reap a huge benefit. Remember, this is your diet, your plan, your life.

To Diet or Not to Diet?

So you think you're fat. Are you sure? Do you think so, or has someone suggested you could lose a few? Has a doctor told you that you could be at risk for high blood pressure or diabetes if you don't take the weight off? Does your mother or father nag you every time you put something in your mouth? Do friends tease you? Do strangers give you that she-would-be-so-pretty-if-she-lost-twenty-pounds look? Or do you just feel fat because your best friend wears two sizes smaller than you? Or maybe you feel unattractive when you pick up a magazine and see the super-skinny frames on the cover models. Is your weight a real issue, or is it that you just don't fit the ultrathin stereotype that is pushed on us by TV, the movies, and magazines?

Just so you know, the models posing for pictures that grace our favorite magazines don't look like that either. They are not as perfect as they appear. Their faces and figures are enhanced on the computer to mask any unsightly blemishes and to shave off any not-so-flattering bulges, presenting us the illusion of perfection. What you see is not real. Honestly, you can buy a computer program for yourself and look exactly like one of those "perfect" models. Or you can see how it's done. The owners of Dove, the soap, have launched a national advertising campaign using normal women with real bodies. On their website (www .campaignforrealbeauty.com) you can actually see for yourself how a lovely, average young woman is taken through a series of computer alterations and made over into a supermodel. I applaud Dove and their commitment to encouraging women to be themselves and avoid comparing their natural beauty to a false image.

It is really sad that so many of us are not comfortable in our bodies. The researchers at Dove conducted an extensive global study and found that women all over the world felt the same way. On their website they say that only 2 percent of women around the world consider themselves beautiful, and more than 50 percent say their bodies disgust them. We all need to work together to change this belief. Each one of us must recognize the beauty we possess, whether it be outward or inward, and we need to stop obsessing about the media's unrealistic standard of beauty – a standard that doesn't even exist.

> **tip** Thin people aren't necessarily healthier or happier.

I'm not suggesting that we stop trying to improve ourselves. We are all influenced by people we admire, and that's not necessarily a bad thing. It's quite natural to copy the hairstyles and fashions of the moment, and to emulate actors, singers, and athletes. But keep in mind that you are an original, not a copy of a fictional creation.

Appraising the Situation

Before you even think of dieting, I want you to ask yourself a very basic question. Are you *sure* you really need to lose weight? Think about it.

The answer might be *yes* if –

1. your doctor suggested that you would be healthier if you did lose weight
2. your parents think you should lose weight
3. your P.E. or health teacher asked you to talk to your parents about weight loss

4. your friends tease you about your weight

On the other hand, the answer might be *no* if —

1. your parents and friends tell you that you don't need to lose weight, even though you see fat when you look in the mirror

2. you are ten or more pounds under the normal weight for your age range

3. your doctor insists that it would be unhealthy for you to lose any more weight

4. you think you should lose weight because your body doesn't look as thin as your friends' bodies (this may not be a weight problem but simply a matter of body structure)

So you've considered it seriously, and you know that you could be healthier if you lost some pounds. Do you have a number in mind? It's great to have a goal, but sometimes we choose a number based on what a friend weighs and it's not realistic for our body. If you get to where you look and feel great but you still haven't reached that magic number, you may want rethink your goal.

And speaking of numbers, don't get too hung up on weighing yourself daily. Personally, I don't like scales. What we weigh at any particular time depends on a variety of factors: our hormonal balance, what we had for dinner the night before, and how much liquid we're holding. Psychologically, it's a bad idea to check with the scale. If you weigh light, you celebrate with pizza, and if you weigh heavy, you drown your sorrows in ice cream. Let's face it, this is a no-win situation. Judge your weight-loss success by the way your clothes feel. When the pants get baggy and you need to go shopping for a smaller size, you *know* you're on the right path.

How Did the Fat Find Your Body?

One day, all of a sudden, we found out we're oversized. We looked in the mirror and screamed. How did this happen? Some people say it's simply a matter of eating too much and not exercising enough. That's part of it, but what about your friend who devours a Big Mac and a large order of fries daily for lunch, never misses dessert, snacks constantly, and doesn't have an inch to pinch? I have a friend like this, and all I can say is, "It's not fair." Not that it helps, but we do know that there is really more to weight loss than calories eaten. Being overweight is a complex condition that is caused by several factors: heredity, unhealthy learned behaviors, personal food choices, puberty, individual body metabolism, emotional environment, inactivity, and lack of knowledge. Let's take a look at each of these.

HEREDITY

It's widely accepted that you inherit the tendency to be either fat or thin from your mom and dad. The fact is that if one parent is overweight, there is a 40 percent chance that you will be too. If both parents are heavy, your chances double to 80 percent. If you are reading this and looking at your pudgy parents in the other room, don't throw up your hands in dismay. There is still hope. You are not doomed to wearing baggy pants and oversized shirts forever. There is no question that those family genes may be waiting in the wings to find you, but there are other very real possibilities that can alter your future.

Consider your parents' habits. What do they eat and drink daily? Do they mostly like steak, fried chicken, sausage, bacon, gravy, biscuits, and chips? Do they often go for second and third helpings? Do they snack on buttered popcorn and ice cream before going to bed? How often do you see them take a walk or ride a bike? Do they drive around the mall to get the closest parking spot or take a place farther away just for the exercise? You see where I'm going with this? It may not be their genetic material they passed along, but rather their daily habits instead.

UNHEALTHY LEARNED BEHAVIORS

Let's face it: We come into this world with both a genetic code and with a family that sets the stage for early lifestyle behaviors. Our parents may not be the best role models when it comes to healthy eating. They may not know a lot about nutrition. Your mom may prepare greasy (but tasty) food lathered in gravy, and she may bake the best buttery muffins in the world. Without intention, you may be eating too many of the wrong kinds of foods. However, we shouldn't blame Mom or Dad for cooking the way they were raised. I'm sure they have no idea they're contributing to your weight gain. After reading this book, you can retrain them. Or, if not, you have other alternatives. Take smaller portions so your Mom won't feel slighted, or go light on the butter and gravy. Even Mom's home cooking is doable if you watch other high-fat foods at meals.

PERSONAL FOOD CHOICES

Your parents decided what you ate up to a certain age. Now you have your own food preferences. It seems that some foods always rank high on the teen list: hamburgers, French fries, pizza, chips, ice cream, candy, and doughnuts. Am I close? I'm not saying that you don't eat other foods as well, but these high-fat foods often seem to crowd out healthier, lower-fat fruits and vegetables.

Maybe you never thought about it before, but too much fat in foods creates too much fat in the body. It's not the only way fat finds you, but it's one of the easiest to spot and one of the first suggestions that nutritionists offer when advising a person how to lose weight. Switching from some of the favorite high-fat favorites (like a hamburger) to lower-fat choices (possibly the barbecued chicken sandwich) is one change you can make to lose weight. I'm not suggesting that you eliminate all of your favorite foods from your diet. You wouldn't anyway, right? Just know that some foods will help you to lose fat and others will help you get fat.

PUBERTY

The teenage years are a period of rapid growth and major bodily changes. Your hormones are surging and emotions run high. You may often feel confused, insecure, and scared about the changes you're going through. Boys are luckier than girls during puberty. They increase their muscle mass and grow taller, often losing their "baby fat." By contrast, girls start producing more estrogen, which brings on their periods and with it, unfortunately, the tendency to store fat. You may have been a stick in fifth grade and now your hips have padding and your breasts are filling out. It's all quite normal, but it can seem like you're living in someone else's body. If it helps, know that you are not alone. All your friends are right there with you. Talk to your mom or a supportive teacher if you're anxious or uncomfortable with your changing body. *FYI: Cutting down on sugar and increasing exercise can help normalize the hormones and reduce some of the stress.* I realize that when you feel fat you may want to seriously cut down on food, but these years are also a time when nutrition is crucial for your health and well-being. Don't stop eating. Read on.

INDIVIDUAL BODY METABOLISM

The way the body makes and burns fat is complicated. One thing we do know is that all bodies don't react the same. Some people store fat more easily (most women) and some burn calories at a faster rate (most men). But there are also metabolic differences among girls and women, boys and men. You see this all the time. You go out with friends who inhale everything in sight and they don't gain an ounce while you walk past a Krispy Kreme and watch your hips balloon. We can complain about the unfairness of it all, or, better yet, we can make some simple lifestyle changes that will help us rev up our own metabolism. Not that we will ever be able to eat like our skinny friends, but it will help us on our quest to lose weight.

EMOTIONAL ENVIRONMENT

Scientists do not agree which is more responsible for causing people to be overweight – heredity or environment. Since they both play a part, who really cares who wins the debate? You now know that you were born with a specific genetic blueprint and with a unique metabolic propensity, and there is little you can do about that. But your environment is something over which you have some control. Well, maybe not when you were growing up. Your mom and dad pretty much determined what and when you ate. Their influence was strong. If your diet was reasonably varied and well balanced, it's more than likely you will be of normal weight and size. However, if your parents preferred mostly high-fat foods, encouraged you to clean your plate, and rewarded you with cakes and candy, there is a stronger chance that you might be overweight.

If the person who raised you withheld food as a punishment or rewarded you with your favorite foods, it may have influenced your attitude toward eating. Do you remember being promised an ice-cream cone if you cleaned your room? Or was it common that you were denied dessert because you didn't eat your peas? I'm embarrassed to admit that I used bribery with my own children. So don't be too critical of Mom or Dad. My point is that you may want to think about whether or not you do this to yourself. When you have aced the math test, do you celebrate with a special dinner or an extra dessert? And how about the day someone told you that your pants were splitting at the seams. Did you soothe your sadness with a large pepperoni pizza?

Food can be a quick fix for anger, loneliness, boredom, frustration, and stress. Just being a teen is stressful. Look at the problems some of you face: homework, grades, relationships (parents and peers), divorce, drugs, alcohol, acne, the threat of HIV/AIDS and other STIs, boredom, the destruction of the environment, war, and your future. Too much stress over too long a period of time can make dieting difficult. And if several of these issues are tugging at you, this is no time to add another one, like trying to lose weight. I would advise you to talk to someone – a counselor, teacher, parent, aunt/uncle, or minister. Get help, and when your emotional environment has eased up, then you can think more seriously about losing weight. There is only so much you can tackle at one time.

INACTIVITY

If there is one magical way to lose fat, it is increasing your general activity level by moving around more and exercising regularly. Physical activity is one of the best ways to speed up your metabolism and change your body chemistry from fat *storing* to fat *burning*. I know many of you hate P.E. and despise sweating. But there are many fun ways to exercise outside of school programs. Just walking twenty minutes more than you normally do each day helps. Walking doesn't cost anything, and you don't have to wear a special outfit. Also, if you're not ready for exercise, know that just moving your body helps to burn additional calories. Take the stairs instead of the elevator, use your feet instead of the car to get around, bike rather than drive, or dance in your bedroom to your favorite music. Little extras like these can take off half a pound a week without your doing anything else. Move it to lose it!

LACK OF KNOWLEDGE

Maybe you are not aware that what you are eating and how much you are eating is putting on the pounds. Maybe you don't know that there is an easy way to change your habits. For example, did you know that the super-sized meal that you order at the fast-food restaurant has in it the total number of calories you should be eating in an entire day? Did you know that many of the salads at these same establishments contain more calories than a normal hamburger? Did you know that the white Alfredo sauce you so love has oodles more fat and calories than the red marinara sauce?

> **tip** Did you know that if you cut one tablespoon of butter off your toast and one tablespoon of mayonnaise off your sandwich each day, you could lose twenty pounds a year?

There may be many things about food and eating habits that you just don't know.

Health Concerns for Being Overweight and Being Underweight

One of my goals in writing this book is to help you find a weight that you're comfortable with and can maintain easily. Being either extremely overweight or extremely underweight comes with risks. However, there is a wide range of variability in what is considered "normal" weight that I'm not sure can be measured by a height-and-weight chart. When you fall far outside the "normal" range for weight, there are health consequences, some more mild than others, and some that won't even show up for decades.

Risks of Extreme Over- and Underweight

RISKS OF EXTREME OVERWEIGHT	RISKS OF EXTREME UNDERWEIGHT
High blood pressure	Stunted normal growth
High blood cholesterol	Retarded bone development
Diabetes	Delayed or stopped menstruation
Heart disease	Delayed sexual maturity
Stroke	
Arthritis	

But I'm Not Motivated

If you are not ready to lose weight, don't. If you have not made a commitment to changing your eating habits and you're only going through with it for Mom and Dad or because your friends are teasing you, the time is not right. You will either fail and feel bad or you will lose the weight and gain it back again quickly. Until you are ready to do this for *yourself*, don't even start. It's healthier to avoid falling victim to the yo-yo cycle of lose, gain, lose, gain and to wait until you're really motivated.

On the other hand, if you read this book and are struck by some things you can change easily that will improve your health, like snacking on fruits and vegetables or replacing one soda a day with water, it may just motivate you to look for other ways to lose some pounds. Often, changing the behavior first and feeling better will give you the motivation to continue. Everyone thinks motivation has to come first, but that's not always the case. Sometimes it's a change in behavior that leads to motivation.

Girls' Special Diet Dilemma

When I was growing up there were many things I didn't understand about my body – and was afraid to ask. This was more typical of my generation than yours. We didn't talk openly about things like sex, pregnancy, and contraception. This may seem really weird to you, but we very rarely mentioned our periods, even to our best friends. You probably hate to hear your parents say, "In my day…," so I apologize. But I do want to make the point that this generation talks more freely about topics that once were taboo, and that's great. The teenage years are scary enough. When you don't know what's going on with your body and you don't feel comfortable asking, all sorts of strange thoughts go through your mind, often blowing minor issues into major problems.

Even though communication has improved over the years, there are some subjects that are not written about or are brushed over in the media. This is true in the area of teenage dieting. I keep checking teen magazines to see what other nutritionists have recommended for teens about losing weight, and there's nothing. All I find are articles on fashion, makeup, relationships, and sex – but nothing on weight loss. What's the problem? Young girls and guys need to know how to diet safely, and they need to know that dieting differs drastically between males and females.

Female weight loss is affected by more variables than male weight loss. It is really true that girls gain weight more easily than guys and shed

17

pounds more slowly. It is also true that some girls have it easier than others, and even for the same individual, losing fat may be more difficult at certain times of the month than others. Let's consider these points in detail, one at a time.

Girls Naturally Carry More Fat than Guys

The female body is different from the male body. My guess is you've already noticed! Women's bodies are wonderfully made to carry and nourish a baby, regardless of whether or not we are having one. From our first period (menarche) to our last (menopause), our body's composition and our female hormones continuously prepare us to carry on life. This basic difference between females and males, as unique and miraculous as it is, makes it easier for us to put on weight and harder for us to lose it.

From the day a baby girl comes into the world, she is disadvantaged in terms of fat. **The female body has almost twice as much fat as the male.** While guys carry around more muscle (which burns calories), girls store more fat (which doesn't burn calories). Muscle tissue burns five calories per pound more than fat tissue. This means that if you ate the same foods as your guy friend or brother, and he maintained his weight, you would gain weight. Likewise, if you were to maintain your weight eating the same food, he would tend to lose weight. **Never diet with a guy.** It's too defeating.

When you read Chapter 6, concerning exercise, you will see that girls can increase their muscle mass and burn more calories. This doesn't mean that you will end up looking masculine – you won't. Your female hormones will prevent that. But building more muscle and raising your metabolism can give you an edge in taking weight off and keeping it off.

Girls Make Fat Easily

The female body has a high percentage of slow-burning fat tissue, which is necessary to the survival of the species. And even though most of us are not thrilled with this fact, it helps us to understand why our bodies fight so hard to hang on to weight when we are trying desperately to lose it. Our fat is so linked to childbearing that when a female's body fat falls below 17 percent of her total weight, she will stop having periods and will no longer be able to get pregnant and carry a child. Whether we like it or not, the female body is designed for motherhood.

You probably know girls who have stopped having periods when they get too skinny. You also may have noticed that they don't have any curves, or hardly any body fat. Many of them look much younger than they are, probably like they did in middle school. This is reversible. When they get to a more normal weight, their periods will resume. Unfortunately, some damage has already occurred while they were underweight, including the loss of bone mass, which will pose an even greater concern many years later.

BEST FOODS TO EAT

Estrogen is the female hormone that directly affects shape and fat distribution. The more estrogen your body makes, the more weight you will hold on your hips, thighs, and breasts. Some people refer to this as a full-figured body; others call it an hourglass figure. The bad news is that this shape makes it easier for you to gain weight and harder for you to lose weight. The good news is that a curvier look is supposedly coming into vogue, and I personally know many guys who prefer a healthy and fit girl to a walking skeleton.

Let me tell you another fact about estrogen. As you may know, it is primarily made in the ovaries. However, you may not know that estrogen can also be made from the fat in our bodies. If you have more fat on your body, you are going to make more estrogen, which, in turn, will make more fat. See the problem? Once you start gaining weight, the body becomes a virtual fat-making machine. Here's the cycle:

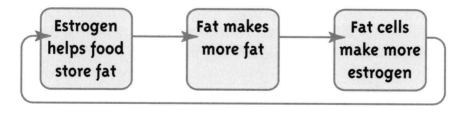

Estrogen helps food store fat → Fat makes more fat → Fat cells make more estrogen

Does this idea make it more clear why it is harder for girls to lose weight, especially those who already have more fat on their bodies? The body is actually working against you. While you're struggling and think you don't have willpower or self-control, your body just wants to go on and make more fat. We often blame ourselves when it's our physiology that's fighting us. I haven't told you this so you can throw up your hands in despair. You really *can* succeed at losing weight. I just want you to be aware that weight loss is difficult and that some of you *do* have to work harder. But with the right plan you too can reach and maintain your ideal weight.

Let me give you a few quick tips that are especially important if you have a full-figured body:

1. **Watch high-fat foods.** Fatty foods are stored faster than other kinds.

2. **Eat high-fiber foods.** Fruits, vegetables, and whole-grain cereals, breads, and pastas will help to lower estrogen levels in the body and assist in removing fat.

3. **Eat small meals more often.** Too much food at one time turns to fat.

4. **Exercise regularly.** Build muscle and burn fat.

Female Hormones and Cravings

A female's appetite appears to fluctuate with the ups and downs of her hormones, both estrogen and progesterone. Estrogen seems to curtail hunger, while progesterone sparks it. After ovulation, which is halfway through the menstrual cycle (for most girls this is two weeks after the start of their period), estrogen levels fall and progesterone levels rise. When this happens, you may want to eat more than normal, and you may find you crave particular foods, like chocolate or salty pretzels. Have you noticed that a few days before your period you're drawn to foods that you can normally resist?

Food cravings may be caused by hormones, but there are other possible reasons why we raid the refrigerator. Being overweight itself often results in eating binges, due to either physical causes (blood-sugar imbalances or an insulin response) or psychological causes (food makes me feel good). Still other possibilities may include a lack of vitamins or minerals and poor eating habits (unhealthy foods and too much sugar). Do any of these conditions apply to you? Look at the chart below for ideas on how to deal with uncontrollable cravings.

Controlling Cravings

Female hormones — Sometimes just changing your diet can normalize hormonal-based cravings. If you are eating three meals a day and you cut down on fat and sugar, these cravings shouldn't be as strong. If they continue, you may want to talk to a health-care professional who understands women's hormones or to a nutritionist. Exercising regularly helps.

Other hormones — An imbalance of hormones, like of insulin, may result in hard-to-control cravings. If you overdo the sugar, the insulin response makes you crave even more sugar. If you starve yourself or even if you pig out, the same insulin response may cause you to overeat. Obviously, the way to calm insulin is to control your eating by not skipping meals, by not eating too much at one time, and by monitoring sugar intake.

Being overweight — Losing weight by itself often minimizes cravings. I won't say that they will be gone forever, but they may become more manageable when you reach your ideal weight.

Vitamin and mineral deficiencies — When your diet is poor or if you don't consume enough calories, it's easy to wind up with major nutrient deficiencies. The best plan is to eat a variety of foods, but it may also be a good idea to take a low-dose multiple vitamin/mineral supplement. It won't make up for a bad diet, but it may help fill in the nutritional gaps.

Emotional triggers — We often numb our feelings with food. Emotional triggers are more of a challenge to figure out and overcome because the underlying reasons for overeating may not be obvious. Consider the possibility that you may turn to food when you are bored, anxious, frustrated, or feel lonely or unloved.

Female Hormones and Weight Loss

In the second half of the menstrual cycle, when progesterone is more dominant, physiological changes take place that tend to make dieting harder or downright impossible. Some girls retain water, so they feel bloated and fat, their fingers and stomach swell, and their breasts are sensitive to touch. Maybe you have noticed that in the week before your period you often weigh several pounds more than you expected. Don't stress out. This is common. It just means you've gained water – not fat.

Retaining water is devastating to a dieter. Even if you tell yourself that it's only water weight, emotionally you feel like a failure. During that week, relax, be especially good to yourself, and by all means don't go near the scale. Know that in a few more days the bloating will pass. Weight loss is a marathon, not a sprint.

If you are prone to water retention, there are some practical things you can do to keep it under control. You can watch the amount of sugary and salty food you take in, you can drink plenty of water, and you can eat small meals regularly.

The Pill and Weight Gain

The oral contraceptive pill makes it easier for you to retain water and also makes it easier for your body to convert food into fat. For most people, this means that if you are maintaining your weight on 2,500 calories per day and you start taking the Pill, you will have to reduce your food intake by 10 percent, or 250 calories per day. There are other side effects of the Pill, too. If you experience *any* symptoms, please tell your doctor. You may know this already, but smoking cigarettes and the Pill do *not* mix. Smoking is not a good idea for a host of reasons, so either don't ever start smoking or find a way to stop while you're young. You will be grateful you did.

Inability to Handle Carbohydrates

Everyone would like to find a medical reason for carrying around too much fat. When you go to the doctor for a checkup, you pray that she or he will discover something wrong with your thyroid. I'm sorry, but rarely do the tests detect a medical reason for being overweight. I do realize there are clinics out there that will diagnose you with a condition and sell you a pill or a procedure to help you lose weight. Please, have your parents check them out before you do anything drastic. Not everyone has your best interests at heart, and some treatments are far worse than losing weight.

> **tip** Don't overeat. Your body can only process about 500 to 900 calories at a time.

There is something noninvasive, safe, and easy that you can try for yourself. Researchers have found a metabolic irregularity in some obese teenagers and adult women that causes them to store fat readily. Some females cannot process too many carbohydrates (breads, rice, beans, and pastas) at one time. Although eating too much of any food causes weight gain, certain women cannot handle large amounts of starchy foods in particular. Whether this condition causes obesity or obesity causes intolerance to carbohydrates isn't clear. Are you eating primarily carbohydrates (breads, rice, pasta, cookies)? Try adding a protein to each meal and snack. Good nutrition means mixing a variety of foods, including a balance of protein, carbohydrate, and fat.

3 Why Most Diets Fail

Strange as it may sound, many teenagers don't have a real weight problem until they diet. When you start on the roller coaster of diet, gain, diet, gain, you set up a condition in your body that makes it harder to lose and easier to gain weight. This is why I feel strongly that if you are not ready to lose weight *for yourself,* then please wait until you *are* ready, and save yourself the heartache of repeated failure.

> **tip** **Repeated dieting may lead to obesity.**

I've seen fad diets come and go and even tried a few myself. Let's see – there was the grapefruit and egg diet, the vinegar/chili pepper diet, the rice diet, the Subway sandwich diet, the high-protein diet, the low-fat diet, and (the latest craze) the low-carbohydrate diet. It doesn't take a medical mind to fashion something new. Weight loss sells. Make up something that sounds relatively reasonable, promise that people will lose twenty pounds in two weeks, and you're on your way to becoming the next diet guru.

I'm constantly amazed that people go back to the same weight-loss program after they have regained their weight. They lose a chunk of extra pounds the first time around by following the latest book or joining a commercial program, but then after getting off the program the weight creeps back on, for some people in a relatively short period of time. So why go through that torture again? I've said it before and I'll say it again: Most fad diets and company plans are doomed to fail for one very good reason. They teach you how to diet one way – their way. You're either "on" the program or "off" the program. They don't give you the tools you need to maintain your weight for the rest of your life. The more structured and confining the diet, the more likely it is to fail. A successful diet must be flexible. In other words, instead of you fitting into a plan, the plan needs to fit you.

tip The faster it comes off, the faster it will come back on.

Skipping meals, cutting out all fat or carbohydrate, drinking protein shakes, and gulping down diet pills and vitamins are common strategies for speeding up weight loss. Each comes with its own set of problems. Here are a couple of hints about trying something new: If the advertisement promises that you will lose ten pounds in the first week or thirty pounds in a month or something else that sounds to good to be true, guess what – it is. *FYI: Realistically, you can only lose about two pounds of fat per week.* Rapid weight loss comes from water loss or loss of muscle mass, not from loss of fat.

Skipping Meals

Many teens and adults think that if they skip breakfast or don't eat all day, they will lose weight or control their weight. This is one of those ideas that sounds reasonable. You save all those calories throughout the day and then feast at night. But scientific studies have shown that it just doesn't work that way. Let's say you plan to eat about 1,000 calories a day in order to lose weight (definitely too low for a growing body – but for the sake of the example, let's use a round number). The studies show that if you spread those calories throughout the day, you will lose weight. However, if you eat them all in one sitting, not only will you *not* lose weight, you may actually *gain* weight.

Skipping meals has the same effect as starving the body. It slows the metabolism by about 3 percent. You may not know this, but you actually burn calories by digesting and absorbing your food. I know your mornings can be quite frantic as you're trying to get out the door, but if you are serious about losing weight at least grab an apple and some nuts, a piece of whole-wheat toast  with peanut butter, or a bagel and cream cheese. The car-bohydrates will give you instant energy and the pro-tein will sustain you until snack time. The bottom line here is that you can lose pounds faster and take in more calories by eating several small meals through-out the day.

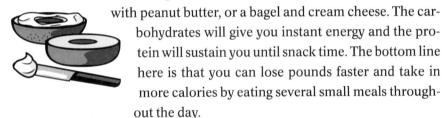

The body operates best if you don't go for more than five hours with-out eating. When you stretch out the time between meals and snacks by too long, you deplete your blood sugar, lose energy, and can't think clearly. Your hunger mechanism switches into high gear and you're pre-pared to eat the next thing in sight that closely resembles food.

The Very-Low-Calorie Craze

The trendy diets that continually pop up usually involve a form of semi-starvation. I found one on the Internet by accident. A beautiful singer (whose name I will not mention, but she's gorgeous, with an extra-ordinary, curvaceous figure) is said to have trimmed twenty pounds for a movie by drinking water mixed with lemon, maple syrup, and cay-enne pepper. This dangerous approach is a prime example of a very-low-calorie diet. Not only does it cut calories, but it almost eliminates them entirely.

Trying to live on diet lemonade, or celery and apples, or diet soda and lettuce is unhealthy for anyone, but especially for teens who need specific nutrients to support these important growth years. Don't listen to the self-proclaimed diet experts who tell you that by following their plan you are cleansing your body of toxins or curing asthma symptoms. You're not. With diets that restrict calories to under 1,000 per day, you are depriving your body of vital nutrients, slowing down your metabolism, losing lean muscle mass, and compromising your immune system. You may also experience weakness, dizziness, diarrhea, vomiting, and hair loss.

When you severely restrict calorie intake, the organs and glands slow down so the body can conserve all of its energy to keep you alive. Muscle tissue is burned, while the fat hangs on tightly as your last energy reserve. You may be eating less food, but you are not burning it very efficiently, and when you do eat, your body responds by storing calories quickly because the body is uncertain when your next meal is coming. As soon as you start eating hamburgers and fries again, those familiar pounds find their way back on to your thighs – faster than before.

The medically supervised fasting programs that are usually associated with a clinic or hospital fit into this category of ultra-low-calorie diets. Even though doctors prescribe them, they are not without risk. According to research conducted at the National Institutes of Health Obesity Research Center, in New York, hospital-sponsored fasts have the highest rate of sudden-death syndrome. Yes, this means exactly what you think: immediate death without warning. This is a high price to pay for a speedy weight loss. And, quite frankly, it's never been proven that quick weight loss in even the morbidly obese teen is effective for the long term.

When self-starvation is taken to the extreme, you eventually lose your appetite. You can train yourself so well to not feel hungry that you lose your natural internal cues for hunger and fullness. Fortunately, they will return when you resume normal eating, but it's not always easy or immediate. You may have to relearn how to enjoy eating.

Very-low-calorie diets often lead to bingeing. There is quite a bit of evidence that starving yourself or even going all day without eating may send you frantically to the nearest refrigerator or fast-food restaurant. You may think your frequent trips to the cookie jar come from a lack of self-control, when, in fact, they may be your body's way of urging you to feed it properly.

What's Wrong with the Low-Fat Diet?

There's the low-fat diet and the ultra-low-fat diet, and it's important to clarify the difference. The ultra-low-fat diet removes almost all fat from the diet, except a very low percentage. I find going to this extreme unnecessary, unhealthy, and certainly unappealing. Most of the flavor from food comes from fat. A more reasonable approach is the low-fat diet, which keeps fat content between 25 percent and 30 percent of your total daily intake of calories.

Reducing fat intake below 25 percent of total daily calories has not worked out well for losing weight. We found this out in the 1970s and 1980s when the trend was to replace fatty foods with nonfat carbohydrates. Supermarket shelves were packed to the ceiling with reduced-fat cookies, fat-free pastries, lite ice creams, yogurts, and salad dressings. And we ate with the assurance that we could eat and eat and not gain because the item contained no fat. You would think that everyone would be losing weight like crazy, right? Wrong. During the no-fat, low-fat years, Americans were putting on more pounds than ever before. Oops. Looks like the experts were wrong.

It turns out that many of these manufactured foods contain added sweeteners in the form of high-fructose corn syrup (HFCS on a label), a very concentrated source of calories. And when you eat such foods in larger quantities, they, too, will pack on the pounds. The bottom line is you can't eat unlimited amounts of anything, even fat-free foods.

The good news here is that you do need fat in your diet in order to lose weight and for the maintenance of health in general. You actually have to eat some fat in order to lose fat. If you don't consume enough fat, your body systems won't work properly. Fat is important for metabolism, and it is also necessary to allow absorption of the essential fat-soluble vitamins (A, D, E, and K). The bad news is that all fat is not created equal,

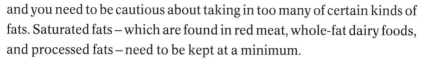

and you need to be cautious about taking in too many of certain kinds of fats. Saturated fats – which are found in red meat, whole-fat dairy foods, and processed fats – need to be kept at a minimum.

Another type of fat that you're hearing about in the news, trans fat, is the very worst. Trans fats should be weeded out of the diet as much as possible. These are the fats found in many fried foods, pastries, and margarine. Many popular fast-food restaurants are now advertising that they no longer cook with trans fats. Labels on foods at the market also advertise zero trans fats. This is a step in the right direction. You might want to support places and buy products that make this transition. Learn to read ingredient lists when you're at the supermarket (more on how to do this is presented in Chapter 7). Trans fats show up on the label as hydrogenated (or partially hydrogenated) oils.

Healthier fats are the oils you find in nuts, fish, and seeds. Olive oil and canola oil are the best for cooking. You often see olive oil at Italian restaurants used as a replacement for butter. Even though healthy fats are better alternatives, they still carry the same number of calories as all the other fats.

Pros and Cons of the Low-Carb Programs

The most recent fad in dieting is to cut down on carbohydrates and replace them with protein and fat. Dr. Robert Atkins started this trend with his top-selling book, *Dr. Atkins' Diet Revolution,* which first came out in the early 1970s and has enjoyed renewed popularity in recent years. His approach was to shun most carbohydrates while filling each meal with steak, eggs, bacon, sausage, cheese, and milk. He was strongly criticized by both nutritionists and doctors for encouraging a diet high in saturated fat, because along with protein foods comes a hefty portion of fat.

Taking this diet to the extreme is unhealthy. The high-protein, high-fat program sends the body into an abnormal state called ketosis. In ketosis, the body burns primarily fat, but as it does, it releases toxic substances called ketones. To protect itself, the body eliminates these harmful chemicals, resulting in a loss of water weight. That's why the scales show a quick weight loss. Because your body is losing water, it is very important to drink a lot of water while on this diet. Besides not working long-term, a high-protein, low-carbohydrate diet overburdens the kidneys and liver, encourages bone loss, and causes bad breath. Yuck.

Since the rise of the original and drastic version of the low-carbohydrate diet, a host of copy-cat variations have come on the scene – the Zone, Protein Power, and the South Beach Diet, to name only a few. They are not as extreme as the Atkins diet, but the thing they all have in common is lowering or eliminating most carbohydrates. Devotees of high-protein, low-carb diets praise this plan because it helps them to lose weight quickly. The downside is that rarely do people maintain this way of eating, and when carbohydrates are reintroduced, the weight typically returns.

Have you noticed how the food industry has jumped on the carbophobia bandwagon? It typically does this with each new fad. Food producers sit in wait for opportunities to profit from people's desire to become thin. It happened with fat-free products and now it's happening again with carb-free foods. Companies who make things like ketchup and cereals and frozen dinners and even chocolate are promoting low-carb versions of their products. I read that Krispy Kreme is coming out with a low-carb doughnut. Is nothing sacred? When I want a doughnut, I don't want a fake, low-fat, low-carb version of a doughnut. I want the real thing: the fat, the sugar, the whole doughnut experience. Even restaurants are offering low-carb meals, and have you seen the thrust of many of the new cookbooks coming out? You guessed it, low-carb.

> **tip** Eliminating any food group (protein, fats, or carbohydrates) is a nutritional disaster.

So, I'm not crazy about the ultra-low-carb diets. They leave out many essential nutrients that teens need for growth, such as B vitamins and calcium and fiber. That's not all. They may make you crabby because you're not getting enough glucose (sugar) to the brain. They may also create wild cravings that will blow all your hard work. Eliminating healthy carbohydrates from your daily eating is not the lifestyle change that I think you need or want for life.

I'm not saying that the low-carb books and programs are totally bogus and don't have anything to offer. They do. Most of them are in agreement that some carbohydrates need to be eaten in smaller quantities. However, all carbohydrates are not created equal. Some raise the blood sugar too fast and are quickly absorbed into the cells and stored as fat. Generally, the low-carb programs all agree, as do I, that it's a good idea to cut down as much as possible on refined carbohydrates such as white sugar and white flour, which are contained in most of the sweet goodies we all love, as well as in white bread, bagels, biscuits, and croissants. These foods also increase your risk for many diseases in later years, like diabetes and heart disease. While many of the books promoting a low-carb plan insist that you totally eliminate white products from your diet, I don't think this is necessary or reasonable. If you keep them to a minimum and eat other healthy foods, you still should be able to stay on your diet plan and lose weight. **Portion control counts big-time.**

There are oodles of what we call complex carbohydrates that are a necessary part of your diet and health. These include fruits, vegetables, whole-grain breads, and whole-grain cereals (no Fruit Loops). These foods not only contain a storehouse of vitamins and minerals; they also offer fiber, most if not all of which has been removed from the refined "white" products. It's the fiber that prevents these carbs from being broken down too quickly. You won't experience the immediate rise in blood sugar, you will feel full faster, and you won't store what you eat as fat so easily.

Most of the low-carb diets, like the South Beach Diet, have phases. The first phase is extremely rigid, eliminating fruits, some specific vegetables, and whole grains. I think this is unnecessary and unhealthy for teens. Once you reach maintenance you get to eat all those "good" carbs. If your mom has the South Beach Diet book and you've been considering trying it for yourself, I would recommend that you jump to Phase 3 of the program, which is more balanced and doable.

Commercial Programs: Good or Bad?

My experience with commercial programs hasn't been too positive. I've worked for some of the top programs and I've seen firsthand the number of people who returned to the same program after months because they gained all their weight back. However that was a while ago, and I understand that many of them have now changed. The focus years ago was on how well you followed a rigid food plan. There was no room for personal choice, no allowance for going out with friends. You had to take each program's food with you to restaurants or sip their drink, while watching your friends enjoy real food. Exceptions were not permitted and you were scolded if you "cheated." Even if you hated their version of a chocolate brownie and wanted to substitute an apple for it, that was not allowed. As a nutritionist I had a very difficult time accepting this, so I told my clients that it would be just fine for them to replace the dessert with an apple. I'm confessing that I didn't follow the rules, but it didn't make sense to deny a person a healthy food in place of one with zero nutrition.

> **tip** Stay clear of any diet that promises incredibly rapid weight loss.

From what I've seen, many commercial programs available today offer greater variety and a certain amount of flexibility by allowing you to eat real food on special occasions. So, for this reason, I do think there is a place for them as a weight-loss tool. Many of the programs provide excellent practical advice on nutrition, changing your habits, and eating in the real word. And, for some people, there are advantages to jump-starting weight loss by using a structured program.

JENNY CRAIG

Jenny Craig is one of the most popular weight-loss programs and it's simple. It provides prepackaged meals with the right amount of calories for you to lose roughly two pounds a week (very sensible). It also offers personal counselors who work with teens one-on-one to help them develop healthy eating habits, learn portion control, and achieve their final goal. As I mentioned, I've not generally been a fan of these programs. However, when I was interviewed for an article by Chrystle Fiedler called "Helping Teens Trim Down" that appeared in the May 2005 issue of *Better Homes and Gardens,* I found out that Jenny Craig offers teens the option of exchanging a regular school lunch for a Jenny Craig meal. The program also provides a "Dining Out Guide" to help teens choose wisely at restaurants. While it is an expensive program and you still have to work out your own lifetime eating plan eventually, for some, Jenny Craig may just be the start they need. Success may also depend on the skills and knowledge of your particular counselor, so if you don't like the first one assigned to you, speak up and pick another.

WEIGHT WATCHERS

I've always been a fan of Weight Watchers because of its proven record of educating clients about caloric values of food, portion sizes, and general nutritional information. Its FlexPoint system is a useful tool that helps both adults and teens become aware of what's in the foods they like and how to pick and choose and still stay within their goal. During weekly classes individuals learn how to regulate their own food according to their lifestyle. Weight Watchers teaches healthy alternatives for snacking, and it offers a support system, which is extremely beneficial for all ages, but especially teens.

Pills and Diet Aids

Pills, potions, and diet aids that guarantee to speed up the weight-loss process come and go because they are an easy sell. Whether they promise to rev up the metabolism or block the absorption of fat, they sound very enticing. But the hard truth is, there are no magic pills that make dieting a breeze. Don't waste your money trying these schemes; they don't work, and they may be harmful.

Just this year, the Federal Trade Commission fined the marketers of several weight-loss pills millions of dollars for claiming their products could help you lose pounds rapidly or reduce your risk for various diseases. Actually, tests suggested that a sugar pill worked better than one of the leading diet pills mentioned. Unfortunately, these products still remain on the shelves even though they are proven not to work. *FYI: When you see a famous Hollywood star talking about how a pill or drug worked for them, remember that they are actors who get paid for making people believe them.*

UPPERS

Most of the diet pills you get from the pharmacy or borrow from your friends are drugs known as amphetamines, or "uppers." These pills were originally prescribed for depressed patients to raise their spirits. They make you feel unusually alert. Maybe this sounds pretty good to you, but there is a dark side. In order to stay "high," you need to keep taking the pills or the effects wear off. When they do, you go from feeling "way "up" to feeling "way "down." The only way to feel good again is to take more pills. This is called addiction. The potential for abuse with diet pills is very strong. Please, if you're smart, you won't start.

APPETITE SUPPRESSANTS

You can go into any drugstore or supermarket and find an entire shelf filled with over-the-counter diet pills. Many promise to take away your appetite, and wouldn't that be great? It would make dieting so much easier; however, a great number of these pills are chemically related to uppers and cause similar reactions. They may not be as strong, but they still potentially have negative side effects like insomnia, constipation, headache, dry mouth, nausea, nervousness, and increased heart rate and blood pressure.

 tip Marketers of diet products care more about their profits than they do about your health.

Some appetite suppressants are decongestants, much like cold and allergy remedies. They may be combined with caffeine (for pep) and a local anesthetic (to dull the taste buds). None are completely safe or free from side effects. Just because you can buy them over-the-counter at the store or over the Internet, don't think they are harmless.

METABOLISM BOOSTERS

Have you seen the ads for pills that will burn calories while you sleep? If you think it's too good to be true, you're right. Products that claim to boost your metabolism while you do nothing to change your behaviors or eating habits do not work, and many have been shown to be extremely harmful. The FDA (Food and Drug Administration) has banned some of these products for containing high doses of a substance called ephedra, which has resulted in high blood pressure, heart attacks, and death—even in teens. No amount of this "natural" ingredient is worth the gamble. *FYI: Just because something is considered "natural" doesn't mean it's healthy.*

DIURETICS AND LAXATIVES

Diuretics, also called water pills, are taken to get rid of extra liquid in the body. Some people use them to lose weight because when they step on the scale it looks like they've lost pounds. Frequently, women take them before their periods to relieve bloating. Don't be fooled by these pills. The scale may show that you're a few pounds lighter, but as soon as you drink a glass of water, that weight is back. Diuretics also increase premenstrual syndrome symptoms. If your body tends to hold water (it's usually obvious if your rings and shoes feel tight), watch your salt and sugar intake and drink plenty of water. I know it sounds strange, but drinking more water helps to relieve the puffiness.

Laxatives clean you out and make you feel "lighter," but the fat does not follow the food when it exits. If you suffer from constipation, there are far easier methods to move the food along. Eat more fresh fruits and vegetables, eat high-fiber cereals (no Frosted Flakes), drink plenty of water throughout the day, and move your body. Teens have been known to abuse laxatives and end up with severe cramping and chronic fatigue.

Mixing the two, laxatives and diuretics, is a really bad combo. Together they can lead to severe dehydration and can trigger electrolyte imbalances that may lead to heart and kidney damage.

STRESS BUSTERS

Supplements that help you fight stress-related weight gain by lowering cortisol, a hormone that is produced when you experience anxiety, have not been proven to work. I'm not an advocate of messing around with hormone levels unless you are advised to do so by a doctor or health-care professional. Raising and lowering hormones randomly can be potentially harmful. Also, some of these products don't inform you that they contain high doses of stimulating substances like ephedra or caffeine.

FAT BLOCKERS

Fat blockers, supposedly a natural and safe way to prevent fat from being absorbed, have been shown to result in minor weight loss. there is a downside. You have to take such high doses that your liver and kidneys are put at risk for damage. There are also the irritating side effects of gas, diarrhea, and an oily discharge. And anything that blocks the absorption of major nutrients like fat or carbohydrates also prevents you from getting important micronutrients like vitamins and minerals.

VITAMINS, TEAS, PATCHES, AND OTHER NATURAL PRODUCTS

Have you read how certain wafers, candies, drinks, or special vitamins, eaten an hour or so before a meal, will curb your appetite? Yeah, and so will an apple, an orange, a small dish of yogurt, a piece of cheese, or a bowl of soup – and they're much cheaper than these special "diet" products.

Bee pollen is something new, at least to me, in the weight-loss field. We used to take it years ago as an additional source of B vitamins and trace minerals, but now it's being hyped to help with weight loss as a "naturally safe" product. Unfortunately, the labels don't contain any warning that bee pollen can cause serious reactions in people with allergies, asthma, or hay fever.

Just because something is advertised as "natural" doesn't mean that it is better or safer than other over-the-counter products. Anyone can claim anything. My advice regarding all of these diet aids? Don't bother.

GADGETS GALORE

You can save a ton of money if you don't fall victim to all the diet gadgets that continually come available. Do not let anyone try to deceive you into thinking their gadget will do anything other than relieve you of your cash. Infomercials and magazine advertisements offer an extensive array of worthless products like appetite-curbing earrings, electrical stimulators, vacuum sweat pants, and spot-reducing belts, lotions, and soaps. *FYI: You can't spot reduce. You can tone certain areas of your body, but you can't choose where your weight will come off.*

When Dieting Takes a Dangerous Turn

Dieting has been taken to the extreme by some teens. You only have to watch TV or flip through a magazine and see bony supermodels and stars like Kate Moss and Mary-Kate Olsen to know that young girls are clamoring to see how low their weight can go. This is a very dangerous trend and one that should be taken seriously. Whether they (or you) have a diagnosed eating disorder or have just gone too far, it doesn't matter. Looking like a stick figure is potentially a very dangerous situation. You may not remember the lovely singer Karen Carpenter, but her secret life of self-starvation led to her shocking death at a very early age. It does happen. There are many books and websites available that contain lots of information about eating disorders. If you think you may have a problem, or if someone has suggested to you that you do, please, please seek professional help.

> **tip** Eating disorders are not really about food and weight loss.

It is true that simple dieting can get out of hand in vulnerable young women and men. However, eating disorders are not really about food and weight loss. Strange as it sounds, they are more about a need to feel in control of one's behavior. An eating disorder may start as a desire to lose weight, but the preoccupation with food eventually takes on a life of its own and becomes an obsession without an end goal. Eating disorders affect males as well as females and individuals of all races and economic levels. This is a very complicated issue that is influenced by a variety of factors – biological, emotional, cultural, social, and familial. For effective treatment, all these factors must be considered.

Anorexia

The most drastic and life-threatening of the eating disorders is anorexia. The term *anorexia nervosa* literally means "nervous loss of appetite." The term is misleading because it is not the inability to eat due to lost appetite that forces girls and guys to starve themselves. Rather, it is a voluntary decision not to eat. The most obvious of the eating disorders, it is characterized by ingestion of minuscule amounts of food, relentless hyperactivity, and excessive weight loss. Although both males and females can get caught up in this unhealthy cycle, it is more common in young girls. In any case, early diagnosis and treatment is critical because anorexia is potentially life-threatening in its later stages. Recovery often takes several years, with many relapses and hospitalizations in between periods of recovery.

If you're already on this spiral of uncontrollable weight loss, I know that your parents' urging you to stop is not enough. When you look into the mirror, you can't see that you're dangerously thin and that your bones are sticking out. You see fat covering corners and crevices of your body where it does not exist. You may even be proud of your thinness because you have achieved something you believe other girls envy. Maybe you aren't ready to hear it yet, but your health – indeed, your actual life – is at risk. Read through the following list and see if anything applies to you.

Could You Be Anorexic?

✗ Do you fear gaining weight when you're already very thin?

✗ Do you consume less than 500 calories a day?

✗ Do you have unusual eating habits? Weigh your food? Cut it into small pieces? Play with your food? Count bites?

✗ Do you avoid family meals and eating with friends?

✗ Are you afraid of food and constantly dwell on avoiding it?

✗ Do you take diuretics and laxatives several times a week?

✗ Do you exercise more than two hours a day, seven days a week?

✗ Are you a perfectionist? Do you need to be the best at everything you do?

✗ Do you set such high standards for yourself that they are almost impossible to attain?

✗ Do you have a hard time sitting down, reading, watching a movie, or relaxing?

 Teenage girls have the worst diets and are most at risk for nutritional deficiencies.

Extreme weight loss is a serious medical problem that results in malnutrition and a host of negative physical symptoms. If you are grossly underweight and have been for some time, you may have noticed some of the following signs:

■ Symptoms of malnutrition

✗ irregular or loss of menstrual periods

✗ dry skin

✗ discoloration of skin

✗ brittle nails

✗ loss of hair

✘ fine hairs covering the body

✘ fluid retention

✘ muscle loss and weakness

✘ intolerance to cold

✘ constipation

✘ digestive problems

✘ anemia

✘ high blood pressure

✘ abnormally low body temperature

I will say this one more time in the hope that you will hear: Self-starvation is dangerous and deadly, and you must get professional help as soon as possible. Check the Resources section, located in the back of the book, for websites that may be of help.

Bulimia Nervosa

The strange word *bulimia* literally means "hunger like an ox." It describes people who overeat enormous amounts of food at one time and then dispose of it by self-induced vomiting or by taking laxatives. They may sit down for a full meal and then top it off by eating an entire pie, two bags of chips, a large pizza, and a gallon of ice cream. The bulimic is a compulsive eater who binges and purges to avoid gaining weight. While the anorexic is obsessed with getting thinner and thinner, the bulimic is primarily obsessed with maintaining her or his weight.

Bulimia is not something teens just invented. It's not a new problem. My mother was bulimic decades before I ever heard the word spoken or saw it in print. I remember her rushing straight to the bathroom after dinner and listening to her throw up the meal she had just prepared and eaten. The family had no idea why she did it. We were sure this was not normal behavior, but at that time no one knew what it was or how to treat it.

Unlike anorexia, bulimia is not as obvious to spot because the individual appears to be of normal weight or slightly overweight. Bulimics are also very guarded and secretive as they attempt to hide their embarrassing behavior. Relationships with parents and friends can suffer as they pull back from being too close. The following are characteristics that describe people who are at risk for this eating disorder.

■ Bulimia occurs most often in individuals who—

- ✗ are in their late teens or early twenties
- ✗ are females rather than males
- ✗ are near normal weight
- ✗ are afraid of getting fat
- ✗ are constantly dieting
- ✗ lack confidence
- ✗ are emotionally insecure
- ✗ are often perfectionists

Expelling food unnaturally from the body on a regular basis can result in a raft of unhealthy consequences. Throwing up food does not allow for digestion or absorption of nutrients, so bulimics suffer from dietary deficiencies and imbalances. Over a period of time, forced elimination can result in the loss of important nutrients and compromised body systems. Relying on laxatives and diuretics contributes to additional problems.

■ The costs of bingeing and purging are—

- ✗ stomach cramps and heartburn
- ✗ chronic indigestion
- ✗ permanently damaged teeth
- ✗ swollen and infected salivary glands
- ✗ irritated and bleeding throat
- ✗ premenstrual syndrome
- ✗ constipation
- ✗ fatigue
- ✗ headache

✗ heart irregularities

✗ high blood pressure

✗ ruptured esophagus or stomach

✗ heart and/or kidney failure

The recovery rate is more encouraging for people with bulimia than it is for those with anorexia. Still, bulimia is not a condition to be taken lightly, so if this section describes you, please get professional help as soon as possible. Don't be ashamed. Getting the attention you need is a very mature step in the right direction.

Compulsive Overeating

Compulsive overeaters, like bulimics, binge regularly. Unlike bulimics, however, they do not get rid of the food immediately by throwing up. They purge emotionally, punishing themselves for being so weak in this area.

It is normal to pig out at times. Many of us gorge at Thanksgiving or family birthday parties or when we're just plain bored. This doesn't mean we are all unstable, abnormal, or emotional failures. The difference between those of us who overeat occasionally and those who do it several times a week is that those of us who do it now and then don't take it personally. We don't berate ourselves. We just brush it off. We're uncomfortably stuffed. So what? We'll eat less tomorrow.

There are clues as to whether overeating is an issue.

■ The clues to problem overeating include—

1. doing it regularly

2. taking it personally (feel remorseful, guilty, embarrassed)

3. hiding the amount of food you eat

Some psychologists think people who overeat are really trying to do something good for themselves. They have problems they don't know how to deal with, so they use food to help them forget those problems and to make them feel better. If this is the case, the overeater needs to find out what is really bugging him or her. Finding a caring professional who can help you sort this out is the best advice I have. Our parents, friends, and school counselors are just not trained adequately to give us the insight we need. Have your mom or dad locate a professional counselor for you. And if you want to share your feelings with others your age, there are websites where you can unload.

Emotional Eating

Emotional eating is something everyone does at some time or another and it doesn't necessarily turn into an eating disorder. Sometimes it just becomes a habit, and habits can be broken. It's very easy to use food to mask any number of feelings, for example –

✗ to cope with unsolvable problems (your parents are getting a divorce)

✗ to soothe anxieties (you're failing math)

✗ to numb feelings (you can't seem to make friends)

✗ to relieve boredom (no one is home after school)

✗ to provide comfort (you hate the way you look)

✗ to celebrate (it's Friday)

I can't list all of the feelings and issues with which you might be struggling. I just know that when I was a teen (or maybe it was when I was a 'tween) every day after school I would scarf down a package of potato chips. I now know I did it for all of the above reasons. I had "issues" with my parents, I hated my body, I had few friends, and no one was around when I came home from school. Sometimes our lives are beyond tough and it's convenient to turn to our all-purpose soother.

> **tip** Overeating is frequently tied to the way we feel at that moment.

Eating mindlessly because we feel a certain way is neither good nor bad. It's just an inappropriate response, and it can be changed. So what is it that sets you off? What triggers your late-night raids on the refrigerator or your after-school eating rampage? I bet if you just think about it, you already have an idea. It's very important for you to get more in touch with these times and your specific feelings.

Now you should write down the obvious instances when emotional eating occurs and the feelings that you associate with it; then, keep the book close by and add to your list the times that you didn't think of at first or that you didn't want to acknowledge. It's often easy to leave something out until it actually happens and you experience that light-bulb moment. Let me give you some examples to spur your thinking. When you overeat for emotional reasons, are you bored, sad, frustrated, lonely, angry, depressed, feeling unloved, or celebrating?

Times when I overeat and why

1. ....
   ....
2. ....
   ....
3. ....
   ....
4. ....
   ....
5. ....
   ....

I know this is like homework, but the difference is *you* are the project and you don't have to turn your work in for a grade. Every paper gets an "A" for effort. I also don't want you to think I'm expecting you to stop your emotional overeating just because you figured out that you finished the chocolate brownies when you were bored out of your skull or mad at your best friend. However, making this connection is a great start to conquering it.

I also urge you to start being kinder to yourself when you do binge. Don't berate yourself and think that you're a bad person because you can't control your eating. Forgive the behavior. Forgive yourself. And know that you are becoming aware and that you are working on this area of your life. As your awareness increases and you start practicing some of the suggestions presented in this book, you will get better. You may also want to share your problem with a close friend or a parent. It's likely that they have done the same thing, and they may be able to support you through it.

If you've just started using food as a substitute for your unresolved feelings, your chances of stopping it yourself are pretty good. The following suggestions may help you take steps to control your behavior. Don't try to tackle them all at once. Take one suggestion – I would go with the easiest one first – then try another.

■ Suggestions for controlling emotional eating

1. **Begin by observing your eating habits.** Pretend you are a reporter doing a story on someone else (it removes the guilt), and write down what, when, and how you feel when you overeat. Do this for a few weeks or a month, and see if you usually overeat for the same reasons or for different ones. There may be more than one trigger for bingeing. Do you overeat every afternoon when the "soaps" are on or late at night when the house is quiet? Do you only attack food when you fail at something or when you miss your dad?

2. **Substitute another action when you are susceptible.** Once you have identified your unique patterns, make a list of alternative things you could do during those vulnerable moments. Here are a few ideas:

    ✗ Call a friend and talk about the situation.

    ✗ Listen to your favorite music.

    ✗ Put on music and dance.

✗ Take a walk in the open air.

✗ Sip on water or make tea.

✗ Deep breathe.

✗ Ride your bike.

✗ Walk the dog.

✗ Rent a video.

✗ Meditate or pray.

✗ Write in your journal.

✗ Take a long, hot bubble bath.

✗ Read an interesting book or magazine.

✗ Punch a pillow.

✗ Cry.

3. **Rearrange your schedule so you aren't faced with temptation.** If you've made the connection between after-school eating and boredom, don't go straight home. Meet a friend somewhere other than at your own home or go to a friend's house. Or go watch football practice, see if you can join a team sport or school club, or take dance lessons or yoga.

4. **Plan one day's eating at a time.** You're probably on a schedule with school, events, homework, and household responsibilities. Think about what you are gong to be doing tomorrow. When will you be eating? And what? Is tomorrow going to be an average day, or might it be one of *those* days when you are going to be faced with the temptation to overeat? Is there anything you can think of now that can change the outcome of tomorrow's events? How can you avoid the inevitable before it's too late?

5. **Remind yourself that there are no forbidden foods.** Anytime we look in the mirror and decide that Monday is the day to start the diet, we think we have to get rid of all the foods we love between now and then. As you read on you will see this is not my approach to weight loss. If there is something you are craving, especially at first, it's better to eat a small amount of it than to feel

totally denied. If your mouth is watering for ice cream and you substitute nonfat yogurt because it is better for you and has fewer calories, you may just end up eating both. Sound familiar? There may be a day when you can easily choose yogurt over ice cream, but *when the craving is strong, go for it,* just limit the amount.

6. **Use the "better than" approach when you can.** In later chapters I will give you examples of foods that have fewer calories and fat grams so you can decide when and how to cut down enough to make weight loss possible. Sure, there are times when you "need" the high-fat food, but when you don't, take advantage of it. When you are truly hungry for food, there are many choices that are more nutritious and lower in calories than others. Here are a couple of obvious examples: An apple is better for you than an apple turnover. A glass of milk is a better choice than a milk shake. Use this "better than" plan when you can, and you may be surprised that you will naturally learn to do it more and more often, especially when you see the results.

7. **Don't eat if you are angry, upset, sad, or overly emotional.** Drink water or have a light soup or some yogurt during these times. Think light until you can enjoy and digest your food.

8. **Be aware of when you are really hungry.** You should only eat when you feel true stomach hunger. Do you know what that feels like? Pay attention to when you haven't eaten in four or five hours and your stomach is growling. Doesn't food taste so much better when you're really hungry than when you mindlessly shovel it into your mouth? When you do eat out of hunger, pay attention to how it smells, looks, and tastes. Sit down (there are still calories in food eaten while standing up or driving in the car). Take slow bites and enjoy each swallow. If it doesn't taste good, don't waste the calorie intake.

9. **Eat with friends.** Many people who are overweight, or who think they are, do not eat in public. Then when they are home alone, they ravage anything that hasn't turned furry and green. Because they feel that people are judging them, they want to

show the world and their friends that they are trying. They don't feel they deserve to enjoy food if they are overweight. Denying yourself fun and the social enjoyment of eating leads to solitary overeating and self-hatred. Go ahead and enjoy eating with others.

10. If you "blow it," so what?

Slipups don't make you a failure. So you planned your day and avoided what you thought would send you straight to the Krispy Kreme drive-through, but it didn't work. Remind yourself that you're still trying to figure this all out. Or maybe it worked last time but not this time. Life was just too overwhelming. Don't beat yourself up. You're practicing at altering a very difficult behavior and today wasn't your best effort. Oh well. Think of a sports star, like maybe Kobe Bryant or Serena Williams. Do they turn in a perfect performance every time they play? Of course not. They're champions, but they still lose matches. What do you think would happen if they gave in to self-doubt every time they played less than perfectly? That's right – they wouldn't be household names. They would never have made it past the junior level of their sport. As they or anyone else who has mastered something difficult will tell you, keep at it. The key is not to guilt yourself into feeling shame and remorse. You're on the path to recovery, and the path is never straight.

Winning the battle against overeating is not easy, but it is possible. It begins with an awareness of the situation, admitting you have the problem, and developing your own plan to change. Once you do this, you are already on your way. You will not succeed overnight, so don't get too discouraged and think you are hopeless. Expect small, short victories at first. Each time you overcome a potential binge, you are one step closer to being in charge of your life. Congratulate yourself!

 # What's More Important than Losing Weight?

I'm guessing that your answer to the question above is, *"Are you crazy? Absolutely nothing is more important than losing weight!"* But I disagree. Feeling good about yourself and your body right now far exceeds the weight issue. You're probably thinking that if you were to lose the weight you would feel good about your body and then you would feel good about yourself. And this is partly true. When you like your reflection in the mirror, you are generally happier with yourself, and this attitude spills over into other aspects of your life. But *FYI: You are far more than just your body size.* Therefore, I want you to consider the idea that you can start feeling better about yourself even before you reach your ideal weight, or even if you never get there.

The plain truth is that hardly anyone is completely happy with the way they look. According to statistics, almost half of teenage girls (46 percent) and more than one-fourth of the guys (26 percent) express dissatisfaction with their bodies. My sense is that the actual numbers are much higher than that. Even those people we imagine as having perfect bodies don't always like what they see. I've heard rail-thin models and Hollywood stars say in interviews that they don't like their thighs or noses or butts. And we say, *"What? Are you kidding? I would give anything to look like that."*

50

It's unfortunate, but we all tend to compare ourselves to the celebrities and superstars we see on the big screen, magazine covers, and TV. We look at their seemingly flawless images and wish we could wave a wand and turn into them. It's very disturbing when the world seems to showcase as the ideal people who have emaciated figures, clear skin, and perfect hair. The truth is those images you see and want to copy aren't always real. I'm not saying that your favorite idol doesn't look fantastic, but generally he or she is not as perfect as you probably think. Photos of him or her are digitally enhanced for magazine covers. Bumps and curves are shaved off the problem spots, and camera angles hide blemishes and flaws we would notice if we saw that person walking down the street. In movies, body doubles sometimes step in when too much skin is exposed, so we're often not even seeing the person we think we're seeing. Let's face it, we are frequently comparing ourselves to something that's not real. That's called a no-win situation.

I'm not saying there aren't beautiful girls and guys with wonderful bodies or that we shouldn't appreciate the time and effort they put into looking good. However, you must recognize that many of these famous people have personal trainers, full-time cooks, nutritionists, and hair stylists. They may exercise or dance eight hours a day to keep their body fit, something that most of us can neither afford nor have time to do. And let's not forget to mention the few who God made naturally gorgeous or handsome, well-proportioned, and gifted. Comparing ourselves to them is also not productive. We need to change our focus from wanting to emulate someone else to aiming to be the best person we can be.

You may think that if you just lost the weight, you would have no more problems and you would be happier. This is called an unrealistic expectation. Everyone has problems. *FYI: Skinny people are not necessarily happier or healthier than you are.* Everyone has issues and concerns that are not dependent on shirt or pants size. I want you to consider the possibility that even if you don't like your body and think you have nothing to offer until you reach your goal weight, you're wrong. You are more than a number on the scale. You are an individual who possesses abilities, talents, gifts, and skills, and if you start focusing on the positive things in your life, you can feel better about yourself before losing weight. Don't think you have to wait until you reach a specific number of pounds before you start living a healthy, productive, and fun life. Start now.

> **tip** Size is not a valid measure of your worth.

Feel Good about Yourself Now

For decades the media has conspired to make you think that you must be a certain size and look a certain way in order to fit in to society. How wrong they have been. Diversity is what makes us unique and wonderful. And finally, at long last, a handful of media moguls are trying to change the message. Have you noticed the Dove soap commercials and billboards displaying normal-sized women wearing only their underwear? What a concept – real women selling real products. This company has done something no one else has even considered. They are giving typical, and not-so-perfect, women public attention and showing how fantastic they are no matter what size, shape, or color they are. Dove has also combined efforts with the Girl Scouts of American to foster self-esteem, specifically among girls between the ages of eight and seventeen. Check out their website, www.campaignforrealbeauty.com. They are sending a long-needed message that beauty isn't only about your outside appearance. It is a combination of all your qualities.

Another nice moment that makes me think times are changing occurred as I watched the 2007 Golden Globe Awards. A beautiful, young woman, America Ferrera, accepted the prize for portraying a not-so-pretty girl (on the outside) on the TV show *Ugly Betty*. In her acceptance speech, she said she wants women to feel worthy and lovable and to know they have more to offer than just their appearance. She also said that we need to stop using the "U" word to describe ourselves. I hope the guys are also paying attention to these wise words. You don't have to be the hunk of the month with washboard abs to be attractive or worthwhile.

Scientific studies have shown that people are more likely to take excess weight off and keep it off when they feel good about themselves. I know this is easier said than done. And I know you're anxious to get to the "dieting" part of the book, but before you plan your food or exercise program, I want you to think about and write down what you like about yourself. It may be hard at first, so start with your most outstanding and obvious features – your hair, eyes, legs, voice, smile, or personality.

Sometimes it's hard to key into your finer qualities. On the other hand, if I were to ask what you hate about your body, you would answer without hesitation. Consider the times when you've been complimented. Does that help? Ask a good, trusted friend for suggestions. Maybe your best features include things you can't see: kindness, generosity, friendliness, artistic or musical skills, debating ability, sense of humor. Write down everything.

The best things about me are...

1. ....
....

2. ....
....

3. ....
....

4. ....
....

> **tip** Don't put off being the person you want to be.

Was making the previous list difficult? Maybe you don't feel all that great about the way you look or about who you are now. Maybe your unhappiness with your body is too overwhelming and it consumes your life and activities. However, it is essential that you know that you have made a decision to work on creating the person you want to be.

Think about some of the people (outside of Hollywood, movies, and TV) whom you admire. Why are they important and what is it you most like about them? It could be a teacher who has inspired you because of her knowledge and gift for making things interesting and clear. It could be an athlete because of his talent and skill at playing tennis or football. It could be an environmentalist who cares about our planet, or a musician who speaks to you through her voice or his guitar. You may respect a writer who transports you to another time and happier place through the written word or your parents who just love and support you for who you are. My guess is that some of the people you most look up to are not found on the cover of a magazine.

What are some ways you can start feeling good about yourself right now? Let me offer a few suggestions:

1. **Learn something new.** Possibly you could start feeling better about yourself by learning something new. How about lessons: voice, drama, dance, piano, or guitar. Check with the parks and recreation department in your city, or inquire at a local bookstore. Both offer classes in all sorts of things, from cooking to travel to exercise.

2. **Join a club.** What's your interest – debate, chess, books, language? If there isn't a club for your favorite activity, start one yourself.

3. **Indulge in some instant gratification.** Maybe something more simple and attainable could lift your spirits. How about experimenting with a new haircut, trying new makeup, or revitalizing your wardrobe? I know. You want to wait until you lose weight to get new clothes. Well, you don't have to redo your entire closet. Find a new blouse, sweater, or pair of pants that helps you feel good right now. Don't postpone taking care of yourself.

4. **Organize your living space.** Where you live reflects how you feel, so maybe you could make over your bedroom to reflect a brighter, cheerier you. Get a new bedspread or bookcase, or organize your CDs, DVDs, books, or collections. Hang pictures of people you admire and images of people doing things you would like to do someday.

5. **Walk tall.** Something that can be done immediately and costs nothing is standing straight and walking tall. At the risk of sounding like a parent, do you stand up with your head held high and your shoulders back? Or do you slump over, looking at your feet and avoiding eye contact? Start acting like you have achieved your weight goal and are happy about who you are and what you're doing. People will wonder what you have done to yourself, and you won't even have spent a dime. As soon as you respect yourself, others will follow.

6. **Help others.** Have you ever thought of volunteering for organizations that serve the less fortunate? I don't think there is anything we can do that is more fulfilling than helping people in need. You can check with your local church, social-service clubs, civic groups, or YMCA. You could tutor a struggling student, watch the child next door, or stuff envelopes for the next political campaign. Teens at my church have gone on trips to Mexico to help build homes and plant gardens. Opportunities are out there. Watch for them.

Broaden your horizons. Try something new. Once you add more variety to your life, eating will lose some of the importance it holds now. If you are serious about losing weight, begin by making your life richer and by feeling more confident in other areas.

Change the Voice in Your Head

Changing habits requires thought and planning. It's important for you to examine your thoughts about your body and about losing weight, as well as your dietary behavior. What do the voices in your head tell you about who you are? Do they build you up or do they tear you down? If the voices in your head are destructive, you need to be more intentional about changing them, just as you are about changing your eating patterns. If you don't, you will not achieve your goal. You cannot change what you don't recognize (an Oprahism). Take time to look at how you feel. This section of the book will help you do that.

> **tip** We can change our lives, but only when we're ready.

Getting clear about what you DON'T like or want in your life will help you make decisions about what you DO want. It is not my intention to make you feel worse about yourself, but I do want you to recognize how you truly feel so you can move on and live a more positive life. The next exercise asks you to write down how you feel about being overweight. It may be difficult to uncover your feelings, so let me start you out by sharing some comments I've heard from other teens. Then you can fill in your own thoughts.

Many teens say: *I feel…*

✗ ugly: I can't wear the latest styles, and the clothes I do wear look sloppy.

✗ self-conscious: I don't fit in with the other girls and guys.

✗ embarrassed: I hate to go to parties or go shopping with friends because they all look better than me.

✗ angry: My mother tells me not to eat fattening things, and then she keeps them in the house.

✗ envious: My best friend is skinny and can eat anything.

✗ frustrated: I want the weight off, but I want to eat with my friends and have fun, too.

✗ insecure: People talk about me behind my back and say I'm fat.

✗ bad: I don't date very often.

Now it's your turn.

How I feel about my weight

1. ....
....
2. ....
....
3. ....
....
4. ....
....
5. ....
....

If you could close your eyes and magically be rid of your extra weight, how would you look? How would you feel? What would you be doing? What would you be wearing? How would your life be different? Try it. Close your eyes and picture yourself the way you want to look. Is it hard? Glance at the following list and see if you can relate to any of these thoughts, and then write down the way you see your ideal self. Besides the ones on the list, come up with your own creative ideas, too.

■ **If I were at my goal weight, I would be . . .**

✗ looking good

✗ feeling good about myself

✗ confident

✗ friendlier

✗ wearing midriff or tuck-in shirts

✗ going out with my friends more

✗ dating more

✗ having more energy

Now it's your turn.

If I were at my goal weight, I would...

1. . . . .

2. . . . .

3. . . . .

4. . . . .

5. . . . .

Has it ever crossed your mind that the reason you haven't lost the weight (even though you've tried) is because you may be afraid it will change your personality, or because you may have to make new decisions about your social life and how people respond to you? This can be a pretty scary thought. After all, you know what your life is like now. You may not like it all that much, but at least there are few surprises. Maybe you think that if you were thinner, you might be –

✗ too different: I know who I am now.

✗ noticed: I don't know if I want that.

✗ friendless: My friends say they like me as I am.

✗ sexy: That scares me.

✗ responsible: I would have to do those things I said I would do when I lost weight.

✗ like everyone else: I like that I'm different.

If you honestly think that the fear of losing weight is preventing you from becoming the person you desire to be, talk to someone about it, like a counselor or your parents. Some of the teen websites listed in Resources section may also be helpful.

Why Do You Want to Lose Weight?

I'm coming to the end of the question-and-answer period. This may seem a bit repetitious, but you're almost done. Have you even thought about why you can't stick to a weight-loss plan? If you have been on any diet, you know that the first few days are easiest because you are highly motivated. You are a tower of strength when it comes to turning down the fries and you easily ignore the chocolate chip cookies in the cupboard. After a few days have passed, the scenario changes. You're sick of celery sticks and protein drinks. You're craving a cheeseburger, and you haven't a clue why you ever wanted to put yourself through this agony.

During these "down" moments, a reminder may be helpful. If you can refresh your memory with all of the reasons why you want to lose weight, your chances of falling into temptation are greatly reduced. I'm not saying it will always work, but even if it works half the time, you're heading in the right direction. It's much easier to control what you eat when you can actually picture in your mind the results of your efforts.

You are more likely to stay on track if you don't lose sight of the reasons why you want to change your life. If you let your mind focus on how good the ice cream is going to taste rather than how good you're going to look and feel when you've dropped a few pounds, it's over.

With this in mind, I want you to make a list of all the reasons you can come up with for wanting to take some weight off. I'm sure you can easily think of a few reasons immediately, and later you may remember more. To start you out, here are some reasons that I have heard from teens. Yours may be similar or they may be different.

✘ I want to look better in my clothes.

✘ I want to walk by a window or mirror and not avoid it.

✘ I want to feel good about myself.

✘ I want to feel more confident.

✘ I want the teasing to stop.

✘ I want to date more.

✘ I want to be more active.

✘ I want my parents to be proud of me.

Why I really want to lose weight

1.
2.
3.
4.
5.

Design Your Dreams

There are mental exercises or tricks you can use that will help make dieting or changing your habits easier. You have just completed one. You thought about and wrote down why it is important for you to lose weight. Take a look at that list again. Read it and make another copy, one you can keep handy and refer to constantly. Read the list in the morning when you first crawl out of bed. Read it at night before you go to sleep. And read it in the afternoon when your willpower is weak and you're craving a chocolate bar. Memorize the list so you can remind yourself any time of the day.

It is easier and faster to achieve a goal if you can picture it in your mind. So the next exercise is to practice seeing yourself as the person you long to be. Go back a few pages and find the list you filled out that describes how you would feel at your goal weight. I really want you to concentrate for about five minutes on this image.

This is how it works. Sit down in a comfortable position and close your eyes. Make sure that no one is around and that you will not be disturbed during this time. Please turn off your radio, iPod, TV, and cell phone. Now breathe in and out deeply in counts of ten. So, you count to ten as you slowly breathe in, and count to ten as you slowly breathe out. Do this about ten times until you feel really calm. If it takes another ten cycles, go for it. Feel your entire body start to relax. Think about quieting your toes first, then move up to your feet, ankles, calves, thighs, bottom, back, stomach, chest, shoulders, arms, neck, and head. Notice that you are relaxing every part of your body. Now that you are totally quiet, I want you to think about your goals and the way you want to look and feel when you reach them. Get specific. What are you wearing? And how does it feel to walk down the street in these new clothes that are several sizes smaller? How do you walk, and talk, and carry yourself?

Are you standing tall and walking like you have someplace important to go? What are your friends (the ones who loved you before you lost the weight) saying? How confident do you feel? See yourself the way you want to be, and believe that in time you will be the way you see yourself. Continue breathing in and out deeply another ten times. Open your eyes and know that you are on your way to achieving your goal.

Thought for the Day

Another technique uses the same lists. This time, write one goal on a small index card. Make it the most important reason why you want to lose weight. You can get ideas from reviewing the list of your ideal self once you lose weight and also the list of reasons why you most want to lose weight. Word your goal so it reads like a positive thought for the day (see the examples below). For a week, carry the card with you wherever you go. Then, the following week, make up a new card with another goal, and carry it with you wherever you go. Continue until all of your goals are used up, and then start over or make up some new ones. If you have trouble coming up with positive thoughts, here are some suggestions:

- ✗ I feel great about myself.
- ✗ I like who I am.
- ✗ I look good.
- ✗ I have a lot of energy and I'm active.
- ✗ I am confident.
- ✗ I'm healthy.
- ✗ I'm in control of what I eat and drink.
- ✗ I like healthy foods.
- ✗ I'm getting better and better each day.

I like who I am.

Create a Goal Board

A goal board is something that I have found to be useful in helping me realize what I want out of life. It expresses in pictures and words things that you would like to do or qualities you would like to embrace. You make it yourself as a reminder of your ambitions, dreams, and wishes. I'm not a crafty type or artistic person at all, but this project is easy to put together. Get a piece of poster board, any size you want. Mine was twenty-two inches by twenty-eight inches, but it can be much larger. Go through a stack of your favorite magazines and hunt for pictures, words, or phrases that express who you are and what you want to do or be. Cut them out and paste them on your goal board in any fashion you want. There is no right or wrong way to do it.

I'll tell you what mine looked like. In the center I had pictures of my family, so photos can work too. I found words like "together," "love," "support," "fun," "peaceful." In one corner I had health goals: pictures of cereals and fresh fruits and vegetables, like carrots. I sprinkled this area with images of active women – women walking, swimming, playing tennis, and dancing. The phrases I chose for this part of the board included "love your body," "fit and trim," "energy blast," and "go for it." Since I wasn't ready for a real career at the time, I didn't have any pictures of me doing any specific job-type tasks. What I did want in my future was travel, so I added pictures of airplanes, beautiful hotels, and scenes of Paris and London and other exotic places I wanted to visit someday. To express my career goals I used phrases like "enjoy life," "brilliant achievement," "quality work," and "always improve." My faith has always been a major part of who I am, so I peppered the collage with words like "God is love, "prayer," and "ask and you shall receive." Get the idea?

Looking at your goal board every day can keep you focused. Add new pictures as you find them, and remove anything that no longer seems to fit. Your life should be active and evolving, so your wants and needs may change. That's good. That's healthy. Oh, let me add that everything on my goal board came true.

Physical Activity and Exercise Are Key to Success

I don't believe there is a magic formula for losing weight and keeping it off, but there is something that comes close, and it is simply to move your body more. If you had to choose between reducing your food intake and increasing your exercise, I would say start with exercise. Moving your body more is critical to speeding up the weight-loss process.

Move Your Body All Day Long

Before getting into a "serious" exercise routine, you might consider just taking more steps throughout the day. You burn more calories walking than you do standing, more standing than you do sitting, and more sitting than you do lying down. So think about your typical day. You don't have to write this down; just go over in your mind what you do on a normal day. How much time do you spend surfing the net or playing video games? How many hours of TV do you watch? When you're on the phone talking to friends, are you sitting or lying down? Do you ride to school or walk (this may not be an option), but how often DO you ride in a car when you could walk? Do you save your steps and take the shortest route to the kitchen? Do you ask your little brother to fetch your notebook rather than getting it yourself? Do you make Mom clean your room when you could help out? If you made some of these small alterations in your daily activity level, you could lose up to a pound a week – without making any changes in your food intake at all! Check the chart on page 77 to see the calories burned just while doing regular tasks.

How about setting a short-term goal to move your body more during the next week? You don't have to revamp you entire schedule, but you should consider what could you rearrange that would add more steps to your day? Here are a few suggestions.

■ **I could move my body more by —**

✗ walking the dog

✗ spending less time in front of the computer or TV

✗ taking my iPod for a walk

✗ helping Mom vacuum the carpet

✗ helping Dad mow the lawn

✗ throwing a frisbee

✗ shooting hoops

✗ riding my bike to the store

Now it's your turn.

What can you do this week to move your body more?

1. ....

....

2. ....

....

3. ....

....

4. ....

....

How Exercise Helps

Moving your body more is a great start. Then, when you're ready, a regular exercise program can really fast-forward your weight loss. There are many reasons why exercise works. I won't bore you with all the physiological changes that occur in your body when you exercise, but knowing something about the practical benefits may convince you that it's well worth your time and effort.

> **tip** If you walk for thirty extra minutes each day for a year, you could lose nineteen pounds.

EXERCISE BURNS CALORIES

The most obvious reason to exercise is to burn calories. When you sit and watch TV or talk on the phone, you are burning about 120 calories per hour. This isn't much when you consider that one scoop of Häagen-Dazs has double that number of calories. Just casually walking through the mall burns 240 calories per hour, so even this minimal activity is an improvement over lounging. Now, if you really get ambitious and decide to clean your room, wash the car, or vacuum the house, you could polish off 300 calories (enough to cover the leftover slice of cake). Increasing your activity level by walking more, taking the stairs instead of the escalator, or moving more in general could mean a loss of an extra pound a week, four pounds a month, or a grand total of forty-eight pounds a year!

You can really see a difference in your body image and fitness level when you start to exercise aerobically. Aerobic activities like fast walking, jogging, or jazz dancing burn up to 400 or 500 calories per hour. Once you find something you really enjoy and do it regularly at least three times a week, you may never have to worry about your weight again. Expending 400 calories three times a week for a year can mean a loss of eighteen pounds.

EXERCISE BURNS FAT

Regular exercise produces enzymes that help your body burn fat. Overweight people produce more hormones and enzymes that help store fat more easily and efficiently. Aerobic exercise is the best way to change the metabolism from fat-*storing* to fat-*burning*. Pills and diet aids and special foods do not burn fat. Exercise does.

> **tip** The more active you are, the more energy you will have.

EXERCISE SPEEDS UP METABOLISM

Exercise speeds up your metabolic rate, so you burn calories faster, even when your body is at rest. Cutting calories drastically (below 1,000 calories per day) has the reverse effect and lowers your metabolism.

EXERCISE BUILDS MUSCLE

Continuous exercise builds muscle, and muscle burns calories. Fat just sits there. The more muscles you have, the more calories you are going to burn even when you're doing nothing. This is why most guys can eat two full meals and still not gain weight (well, some of them). It's also why they can lose weight more easily than girls, who naturally store more fat in their bodies. Building muscles is a good way to keep weight off and enable you to eat more food. Fortunately, it is not unfeminine anymore for women to develop their biceps and quads. We, too, can change our bodies from fat-storing to fat-burning by building up our muscle mass.

EXERCISE CONTROLS APPETITE

Most people notice that they are not hungry after exercising. That's because fat is being released into the bloodstream as sugar, which blunts the appetite. Also, after exercising regularly, the appetite regulator in your brain resets itself, so the body becomes more tuned in to its true hunger needs. In other words, you will be more conscious of your real feeling of hunger as opposed to false hunger signals. Let we warn you that this process takes time to kick in, so when you first start your program you may experience the opposite. You may be famished immediately after a workout. This does change, and exercise will curb your urge to eat.

EXERCISE REDUCES CALORIES ABSORBED

Food passes through the digestive system faster when you are active than it does when you are inactive. As a result, a smaller percentage of your daily calories are stored as fat. For example, the average person processes a meal in about twenty-four hours. In obese people, it may take twice as long, meaning there is more time for the food to be stored as fat. Well-trained athletes keep food in their system for only four to six hours.

EXERCISE HELPS YOU SLEEP

Getting enough sleep helps to keep your weight under control. When your body doesn't have time to rebuild itself because it's not getting enough sleep, your entire hormonal system is thrown off track. Appetite-stimulating hormones are released, and off you go on a hunting mission for sugar. Making sure you get around nine hours of sleep each night is essential for the growing body as well as for weight control – and nothing stimulates sound sleep as well as exercise.

EXERCISE HELPS YOU FEEL GOOD

The hormones released after a vigorous workout give you a wonderful feeling of euphoria, a natural high. Exercise calms anxiety and depression and helps you relax. If you are bothered by a problem or feel overly stressed, a long walk can help to ease the tension and will often provide you with a fresh perspective.

EXERCISE BUILDS YOUR CONFIDENCE

A number of positive psychological changes occur when you confront a challenge and overcome it. Sticking to a program, whatever it is, will give you a sense of accomplishment and boost your self-image. When you feel better about your body and yourself, you will find it is no longer an effort to push your body beyond your comfort zone. You will actually look forward to your activity.

> **tip** You can be thin but at the same time not be fit.

Getting Serious about Exercise

When you're ready to graduate from increasing your general activity to considering serious exercise, you have many options. You might try a sport or activity you enjoy or would like to learn, like tennis, skating, volleyball, soccer, skiing, swimming, or dancing. It's easy if your school offers such a class. If not, check with the YMCA or your local community center. The instructors are usually knowledgeable, and the prices are usually reasonable. Or look in the yellow pages of the phone book. You can find specialized classes for activities like gymnastics, horseback riding, or dance lessons, and some gyms offer special prices for teens.

Maybe you don't know if you will like an activity such as ice skating or karate. Ask if you can sit in on a class first to see if it spurs your interest. However, you can't always know how fun an activity will be until you try it a few times. I started tap-dancing lessons two years ago because I'd wanted to tap since I was four years old and never got the chance. Now I'm having the time of my life. It's a fun way to work up a sweat, and I've made new friends as well.

The Big Three

In the ideal word, the well-rounded individual engages in three types of exercises. I realize we're not all there and not everyone cares. But I am going to mention these so you will be aware of the various kinds and their benefits to your body. If you don't exercise at all right now, anything you do is beneficial and worthwhile.

The three types of exercises the experts agree we all need at any age are aerobic, or cardiovascular, activity, strength or weight training, and flexibility training (a.k.a. stretching). I will gloss over the benefits of both weight training and stretching and spend more time on aerobic activity since it is the form of exercise that will most likely help you lose weight in the fastest way possible.

1. STRETCHING

Stretching helps to keep your joints and muscles elastic and flexible. It's usually done at the end of an aerobic workout, because once you have tightened the muscles via exercise you need to lengthen them to avoid pain. Your ability to reach and bend more easily depends on how limber you are. Whether or not you can touch your toes or do a split has a lot to do with genetics, but you can also increase your range of flexibility by practicing. A bonus to stretching is that it will help you prevent injuries, especially if you get serious about running, playing football or other sports, skiing, or any other intense activity.

There are books, videos, and classes that can teach you how to stretch. Yoga is an excellent way to learn a wide variety of stretching poses. It also helps to relieve tension. Most exercise classes end with a stretching session. Once you learn some basic stretches, you can do them at any time and in any place.

2. WEIGHT TRAINING

Weight training strengthens and builds the muscles. It helps to increase metabolism so that the body will burn calories more efficiently even when at rest. There are many benefits to strength train-ing: It helps to prevent injuries, it tones the body, and it makes you stronger and more efficient for other activities.

There are a variety of ways to build muscle, and some of them need to be learned in a gym or taught to you by an experienced trainer. If you're interested in using free weights (barbells) or working out on weight machines, it's best to be instructed by someone who is knowledgeable. A class in Pilates may offer both machines and props that can help you to strengthen your inner "core" muscles (the muscles throughout your torso). And many sports will strengthen specific muscles – for example, gymnastics, basketball, track and field, softball, tennis, figure skating, soccer, and swimming.

tip The best sports drink after exercise is water.

3. AEROBIC EXERCISE

Aerobic exercise, sometimes called cardio (heart) exercise, is the most efficient way to burn calories and reduce body fat. It simply involves do-ing some activity that speeds up your heart rate and breathing for a sus-tained period of time. The word *aerobic* literally means "oxygen in the air." As you exercise, your heart rate goes up, which carries more oxygen to the muscles so they can work. The body is forced to burn calories to create the energy needed to maintain this process.

Aerobic activities are those that work the largest muscle groups, like the legs and torso. They include fast walking, jogging, jumping rope, bike riding, aerobic dancing, and kickboxing.

To get the maximum benefit from your workout there are specific things you need to know. The activity must be done nonstop for twenty minutes, three to four times a week, and within a specified range of intensity called the "target zone." This is the formula that gives you the greatest benefit. However, if you aren't that serious yet, that's fine too. If you think that ten minutes is all you can handle at first, great. I would rather you start something that you know you will do than push yourself beyond your limit and give up.

For those who are interested in getting the maximum workout, let's return to the concept of the "target zone." This is simply the amount of effort it takes to raise your heart rate to somewhere between 120 and 160 beats per minute while you are doing the exercise. Aerobics instructors or personal trainers sometimes ask you to take your pulse during a class or session to see if you are within the range. If you are interested in being exact about your target rate, here is how to figure it: Take the number 220 and subtract your age to determine your maximum heart rate. You never want to work so hard that your heart rate goes above this number.

If you're sixteen years old, this is your formula:

220 – 16 years old = 204 (your maximum heart rate)

To hit your target heart rate you want to work between 60 percent and 80 percent of your maximum heart rate. To determine this number you multiply your maximum heart rate by 0.60 and by 0.80. When you're exercising within this range, you're burning fat most efficiently. If you overexert, you force the muscles to work without oxygen (anaerobically). You will feel pain the next day and your body will not get the same benefit as it does when you are exercising with air (aerobically). So, for a sixteen-year-old:

204 × 0.60 = 122 (rounded down)
204 × 0.80 = 163 (rounded down)

During your workout, your heart rate should accelerate to 122 beats per minute but not go over 163 for you to achieve maximum aerobic benefit.

Some people get very scientific about this and buy a wrist monitor that will continuously show their heart rate; others like to take their pulse after working out for five minutes to see if they fall within the range. I used to do this in an aerobics class until I got to the point where I knew what it felt like to be working within my target rate.

If all of this sounds too bothersome, don't worry. There is a quick and easy way to figure out your personal range. It's the "can I talk?" barometer. If you can talk easily while, say, jogging or walking fast, you're probably not working hard enough. If you can't talk at all, I would say you're well above your target, so slow down. If it's a little uncomfortable to talk but not overly uncomfortable, you're probably right in the zone.

The First Workout

Suppose that you've decided to try walking fast or jogging as your aerobic exercise. Let me take you through your first day. Wear comfortable clothing and get a decent pair of walking or running shoes. You don't have to pay a fortune for the top-of-the-line shoe made for elite runners. Just get a pair that provides good support.

If you plan to take your pulse to see if you're within your target range, remember to wear a watch with a second hand. It's a good idea to warm up the body before you start by gently bending, twisting, and stretching for about five minutes. Walking slowly is also a good warm-up exercise. Never just start by immediately walking fast or running. You need to let your body know you're about to give it a workout. Don't startle it or force it to do something it's not ready to do. As you're walking, slowly increase your speed. As you walk or run, if your heart is beating faster, level off your pace; however, if you can still talk normally, continue to increase your speed. Even if this means you're talking when no one is with you, it's okay. People will just think you're on your cell.

If you want to take your pulse while your heart rate is up just to see where you are in terms of your target zone, do so while you continue walking. Your pulse is taken either on your wrist, about an inch below the bottom of your thumb, or on your neck, about an inch below your ear. Can you find it? Did you remember your target range? There are faster ways to count your pulse than to wait for an entire minute. You can count for thirty seconds and double it, or, to make it really quick, take your pulse for six seconds and add a zero. So if the number is thirteen and you add a zero, you're working at about 130 beats per minute. You should be right in the middle of your range. This is not as precise a measurement as counting for a full minute, but it's close enough.

How long can you maintain this pace? If five minutes is all, that's fine. If you find yourself becoming tired, go slower for five minutes and then try speeding up again. Remember, the goal is to sustain this intensity for twenty minutes, but if you're not even close, so what? You've only just started and you're learning something new. Congratulations for trying. When you have finished, slow down gradually and end by stretching.

If walking seems too boring, ask a friend to join you or bring your headphones along. If it's definitely not your thing, check out some of the exercise videos, look into a structured class, try bike riding, or skipping rope, or something that interests you more.

Why People Quit

When people drop out of a fitness program, it's usually due to one of two reasons. Either they went at it too vigorously and got so exhausted that they quit, or they didn't work hard enough and got discouraged because it took too long to see any results. Or maybe they just chose the wrong exercise. I guess that's three reasons.

It could be that this has happened to you in the past. You were excited at the prospect of losing weight. You begged your mom for the charge card to buy the right outfit. On day one you excitedly rushed to class and plowed full steam ahead. Moments later, the steam started to evaporate, and you were huffing and puffing and ready to exit by the back door. No, that would be too embarrassing, so you kept it up until your muscles ached for you to stop. You were NOT having fun.

Or maybe everyone in the room had a size-zero body and wore micro-mini tops with skin-tight pants. They have been taking this class for years and didn't even break out in a sweat, while you were dripping after the warm-up. My guess is that this is not the place for you. You have to feel comfortable and at ease with your choice, so check out classes in advance. Who is in the class? What are they wearing? Are there others who don't have the perfect body? If you feel *too* self-conscious, keep looking. (You'll probably feel a little self-conscious – after all, you're trying something new.)

Whatever you start, ease into it. Don't plan on jumping into an hour of vigorous exercise the first time. Get used to the feeling of exerting yourself, but don't push too hard in the beginning. It's better to enjoy what you are doing and build upon it. However, be sure to make some sort of commitment and to stick to something. You may not experience the benefits immediately, but if you hang in there, you will soon feel better, both physically and emotionally.

How Many Calories Am I Burning?

The chart below shows how many calories you can burn doing both aerobic exercise and everyday physical activities for thirty minutes. If you spend less (or more) time doing the activity, adjust the number accordingly.

Calories Burned in Thirty Minutes of Activity*

ACTIVITY	CALORIES BURNED
Aerobics class	210
Basketball	280
Cleaning house (steady movement)	150
Climbing hills (steady pace)	250
Cycling (5.5 mph)	130
Cycling (13 mph)	240
Football	270
Golf (walking)	180
Judo/karate	400
Playing piano	80
Rowing machine	210
Running (a 9.0 minute mile)	400
Shopping	120
Skating (moderately)	160
Skating (vigorously)	300
Skiing (downhill)	200
Swimming (freestyle)	280
Table tennis (recreational)	220
Volleyball (moderate)	100

(cont'd.)

Calories Burned in Thirty Minutes of Activity (cont'd.)

ACTIVITY	CALORIES BURNED
Walking (3 mph)	130
Walking (4 mph)	200
Walking (stairs)	300
Weight training	240
Writing	60

* Based on a person who weighs 150 pounds. If you weigh more, you will burn more calories; if you weigh less, you will burn fewer.

Designing Your Own Unique Diet

Finally we've come to The Plan: THE DIET. As I said earlier, this is not my diet, it's yours. So, what are you going to eat? Surprise! I'm not going to tell you. That is, I'm not going to give you a meal-by-meal schedule to follow for the next week or month. I could. I could tell you exactly what I think you should eat each day, and it would be nutritionally balanced and provide the right amount of calories as well as all the necessary nutrients. However, that's exactly what all the other programs do. Yes, you would lose weight in the beginning, but eventually you would get bored with the weird foods I picked and you would go back to the foods you really like. That's not what I want for you.

The Basics

So here are the steps to your plan:

1. **Start where you are, right now.** Don't shock your body and your brain by adopting a program of eating that is totally foreign to you.

2. **Gather information about yourself.** What behaviors seem to contribute to your own weight gain and prevent weight loss?

3. **Learn about food.** What foods do you eat regularly that are very

high in calories and fat, and which of these could you eliminate? Or what foods could you switch to that would also satisfy you?

4. **Make a plan.** Concentrate more on the short-term goals of the behaviors you are going to change tomorrow than the long-term goal of the number of pounds you want to lose.

5. **Practice the changes that come most easily.** Stay with your initial program for a week or two, and then move on to other foods you might substitute or another behavior you are ready to tackle.

6. **Be flexible.** You can vary your plan daily. You can renegotiate at any time when something isn't working. And if something isn't working, don't blame yourself. You haven't failed.

7. **Take your time.** Real weight loss is a slow process, much like learning a new sport or game. All you need is practice.

In order for you to *keep* the weight off, you must change some of your behaviors. What you're doing now isn't working. Your present behaviors are keeping you from losing weight. You must do things differently. Know that you don't have to do it perfectly all the time. You don't have to just eat healthy foods (although I must admit that would be *my* goal for you). But you must make changes that will support your weight loss and that you can live with. I don't want you to obsess over the number of pounds you are going to lose. That number may change with time. The focus is on your day-to-day behavior.

It's not wrong to have a general idea of how many pounds you want to lose. You may know exactly that magic number or have no idea at all. It doesn't really matter on this program because the focus is more on creating healthier habits that will lead you to a healthy weight. The number doesn't have to be the end result. As you get closer to a weight that feels comfortable for you, it will be clear what that number is. Some people set a target weight loss of, say, sixty pounds and when they've lost forty, they find it's enough. Others may think that losing seventy-five pounds is a reasonable goal for them. When you feel comfortable with the way you look, stop attempting to lose weight and concentrate and maintaining the desirable weight you have attained. Be very careful not to go beneath a healthy weight and become caught up in becoming thinner and thinner. If someone says you're losing too much weight, consider the possibility that they may be right.

Mapping Out Your Strategy

Losing weight is not complicated. It's just a matter of numbers. If you are overweight, you are taking in more calories that your body can burn. Don't let the "experts" convince you that calories don't count – they do. Yes, there are other factors involved in weight loss, but the bottom line is –

TO LOSE WEIGHT — BURN MORE CALORIES THAN YOU EAT

TO GAIN WEIGHT — EAT MORE CALORIES THAN YOU BURN

TO MAINTAIN WEIGHT — CALORIES EATEN = CALORIES BURNED

To gain one pound of fat you have to eat 3,500 calories of food above and beyond what your body can use; conversely, to lose one pound of fat you have to burn 3,500 calories or shave that much from your regular diet. If you did this over the course of one week – if you burned off or cut out 3,500 calories – you would normally lose one pound. Breaking this idea down into a daily goal, if you cut 500 calories a day from what you are presently taking in, you would lose one pound of fat in a week. And if you were to continue doing this, you would lose four pounds a month, or forty-eight pounds a year. Maybe that doesn't sound fast enough for you, but what if you knew that at this time next year you could magically be almost fifty pounds lighter without too much effort? Wouldn't you go for it? If you cut 750 calories a day – or cut 500 calories a day and also burned an extra 250 calories each day by exercising – you could lose six pounds a month or seventy-two pounds a year. How does that sound?

Your basic formula for losing weight:
3,500 CALORIES = 1 POUND OF FAT

Action Steps

Starting is always the hardest part. So to get you going I have a few suggestions for different plans and examples of how you might carry them out. Use any combination, as long as the numbers add up to 500 calories per day. Even this is negotiable. Your numbers don't have to be that exact. I'm only using this as an illustration. In Chapter 8, I'll give you calorie counts of many common foods so you can figure out the values of what you're eating and what higher-calorie foods need to be cut from your diet. And you already know how to burn calories – remember Chapter 6?

■ Plan of action

1. Cut out 500 calories from food.
2. Cut out 300 calories from food and burn 200 calories in exercise.
3. Cut out 200 calories from food and burn 300 calories in exercise.

■ Examples of ways to cut food calories

✗ Eliminate french fries – save 270 calories.

✗ Substitute "lite" ice cream for premium brands – save 170 calories.

✗ Switch from mayo to mustard – save 150 calories.

✗ Order a regular hamburger rather than a quarter-pounder – save 300 calories.

■ Examples of exercises that burn 200 calories

✗ Walk four miles per hour for one hour.

✗ Do a half-hour aerobics class or video.

✗ Walk stairs for twenty minutes.

✗ Cycle at five miles per hour for forty-five minutes.

 tip You cannot realistically lose more than two pounds of FAT in a week.

Getting Started

Your weekly weight-loss goal should be no more than one or two pounds. That is generally accepted among nutritionists as a healthy target. If you are losing more than that, you're probably losing mainly water weight or are losing muscle mass.

Don't get overly enthusiastic and think that if you cut your calories drastically you will lose weight faster. It's true that the scale might show a quicker weight loss, but it probably won't be fat that you're losing. The amount of food and the number of calories that you are able to eat while on a diet depends on your sex, individual metabolism, and activity level. Normally, female teenagers can consume about 2,000 to 3,000 calories a day without gaining weight, and male teens can often eat up to 5,000 calories a day without gaining weight. However, like I said earlier, these numbers can vary. To lose weight, you need to go below this number. **However, under no circumstances are young women to eat less than 1,200–1,500 calories a day or young men to eat less than 1,500–1,800 calories a day.** Not only is this unhealthy and unsafe, but you won't lose fat any faster.

There are several ways to start making changes in your diet. And you get to decide which works best for you. I always say start with the easiest first.

1. Cut down on the amount of food you eat. Start by immediately taking two to three bites off your plate and putting them on another plate or throwing them away. If you do this at each meal, you will have saved a bunch of calories. This is one way to learn portion control.

2. Eliminate the foods you don't really like anyway. Sometimes we clean our plates or eat something because it was offered to us and we didn't even like it. What a waste of calories.

3. Replace high-calorie foods with low-calorie foods. This is where knowledge comes in. I will help you make wiser choices after you see which lower-calories foods (that you *like*) could substitute for the ones you are presently eating.

4. Eventually, do all of the above – or vary your plan by doing some of each.

Write It Down to Take It Off

Do you have a clue as to how many calories you take in a day? It's my experience that most people are totally unaware of what they eat and how much. In all my classes I ask students to write down what they put into their mouths for one whole week. And almost everyone comes back in shock at the realization that they eat as much or as often as they do. They previously had no idea, so it's a real "ah-ha" moment when for the first time they get it. Many of them become so enthusiastic that they start eliminating or substituting foods immediately. It's a very motivating exercise.

IT WORKS

Researchers have found that people generally underestimate what they eat by about 25 percent. Therefore, I'm asking you to do yet one more writing task. Keeping a food diary is essential to the weight-loss process. You have to know what you are eating in order to make appropriate changes. In my many years of tracking dieters, I found that the people who kept account of their food intake not only lost weight faster, but they also continued to maintain their goal weight – and maintaining an ideal weight is what it's all about. You must write it down to take it off.

WE FORGET WHAT WE EAT

When you physically put onto paper what you eat, you tune into the fact that you *are eating*. You may be totally unaware of tidbits that pass through your mouth. Many of us eat mindlessly, and we don't even remember the taste and texture of the food we just inhaled. I admit that it still happens to me on occasion, like the other night when I finished off the bag of chips hiding in my cupboard. I was watching TV after an exhausting day and a hurried meal, and I just grabbed that half-filled bag to satisfy some feeling (frustration, exhaustion, boredom). Oh well. I have learned not to punish myself when this happens.

IT'S A TEACHING TOOL

Keeping track of your food intake for one week helps, but it's best to continue until you are well on your way to achieving your goal. Not only does your food diary tell you when and what you overeat, but it also becomes an educational tool. You will learn the caloric value of your food choices. Often, when you realize that your daily hamburger has 900 calories and 92 grams of fat – which is quite a bit for one meal plus more fat grams that you probably need for the entire day – you will likely reconsider whether that is what you really want for lunch. I'm not saying that you won't sometimes make the decision to satisfy yourself with a scrumptious burger, but at least you will know what it is costing you. You can also determine how nutritious your diet is. Is it balanced with proteins, carbohydrates, and fats? You will see how often fruits and vegetables show up in your diet, as well as ice cream and cookies.

IT HELPS YOU PLAN YOUR STRATEGY

Writing things down helps steer your plan. You may spot a particular snack that is adding a huge debt of calories to your day, and then you can decide what you want to do about it. You probably had no idea how many calories were lurking in that double mocha latté. Maybe you never made the connection that your large Coke was stimulating your appetite for sugary foods until you checked your chart and saw how you always bought something sweet shortly afterwards. Knowledge is power, and your food records will give you that power.

IT'S NOT TO GUILT YOU

Record keeping is NOT meant to make you feel guilty. There is no place in the weight-loss process for feeling bad about yourself. If you eat a high-fat food because you can't stop the craving, write it in your record, but don't beat yourself up about it. Write it down, then go back later and rethink how you might handle a similar situation the next time one comes up. You don't have to deprive yourself of any particular food item immediately. However, you may find another food that satisfies the same food urge.

STEPS TO RECORD KEEPING

1. **Enter the food in your chart.** There is a blank chart located on the last page of this book. You can write on it or, better yet, make copies to use, if that's more convenient. Some people create their own chart, one that fits into a favorite notebook. Whatever works for you is perfect. Pick a day to start. (It doesn't have to be a Monday.) Then write down everything you eat and drink for an entire week. I mean, put down every crumb, bite, and nibble that passes your lips. Include the serving size. If it's not an individual serving, like one apple, try to guess the size. It could be 1 cup of cereal, or a large order of fries, or 12 ounces of soda. You will get better at this as you become more accustomed to paying attention to food labels. The first week is a breeze because all you enter is the food. Don't even think about the calories or fat grams yet. And, by all means, don't evaluate your choices. Pretend you are a reporter whose only job is to record the facts.

2. **Figure out the calories for each entry.** After the week has passed, use your chart and the food lists in Chapter 8 to determine the calories and/or fat grams for each entry. Special books and websites (listed in Resources section) are available that provide a more complete list than I have included, but you can use the one included in this book as a quick and easy guide. You will find caloric information on boxes and bags of foods that you eat. Start reading labels. They will surprise you. Especially, be aware of the serving size for what you are eating. It's always a shocker the first time you realize that a small bag of chips, at 150 calories per serving, is actually meant for two people. It's really 300 calories per bag. Back to the task at hand – looking up the calorie and fat content of foods usually doesn't take as long as you might think, because we seem to be creatures of habit who tend to eat many of the same foods for each meal. Most people eat only about twenty different foods a week.

3. **Focus on your twenty favorite foods.** What are the foods you eat most frequently? Use the space below to jot down the main ones you could easily give up or would consider substituting with

another food lower in fat and calories. Also, fill in the calories and fat grams. This is the foundation of your new diet plan.

Foods I Can Easily Give Up

FOOD	CALORIES	FAT GRAMS

Getting Rid of Fat Promoters

There is no doubt about it. Many of our favorite foods add inches to our thighs. Do you recognize some of your own worst offenders on the following list? Fast foods, fried foods, chips, dips, pastries, butter, doughnuts, cookies, lattés, ice cream. Which of the items on the list are big temptations for you? Circle or highlight these foods. How many calories or fat grams do they contain? How often do you eat them? Daily? Several times a week?

Estimate your daily calories and fat grams from your weekly record. Does the number shock you? Can you see places where you could easily make changes? How much do you like these fat promoters? Do you like them more than you want to lose weight? This could be a difficult choice, I know. Which ones could you live without? Are there some you could easily replace without altering your life too much? Sometimes we eat out of habit or convenience, not because we necessarily have strong feelings for that specific food. Write down some of the foods that are replaceable, try living without them for a few weeks, and see what a difference it makes in your diet.

Making Better Choices

Now that you have decided what can go, what are you going to do to replace the foods in question? If you usually order a Big Mac for lunch but don't think it will bother you too much to change, what will become your new favorite? There are actually many lower-calorie alternatives, even at McDonald's. If you eat barbecue-flavor chips when you watch TV and you decide that you could probably try snacking on something healthier, what would it be?

The following chart shows popular fat-makers and suggests possible leaner alternatives.

Better Choices to Help Trim Calories

INSTEAD OF...	CALORIES	TRY...	CALORIES
Big Mac	570	Regular hamburger	260
Large fries	357	Regular fries	270
Chocolate shake	360	Whole milk, 8 oz	150
Wendy's Bacon Burger	570	Wendy's Chili	228
Whole milk, 1 cup	150	Nonfat milk, 1 cup	85
Chocolate cake, 1 piece	400	Angel food cake, 1 piece	125

(cont'd.)

Better Choices to Help Trim Calories (cont'd.)

INSTEAD OF...	CALORIES	TRY...	CALORIES
Taco Bell Beef Burrito	466	Taco Bell Taco Supreme	237
Carl's Jr. Super Star	780	Carl's Jr. Old Time Star	450
Carl's Jr. Fiesta Potato	432	Carl's Jr. plain potato	200
Club sandwich	590	Tuna sandwich	278
Arby's Super Roast Beef	620	Arby's Regular Beef	350
Ice cream cone, large	340	Ice cream cone, small	120
Dove ice cream bar	497	Eskimo pie	170
Sara Lee cheesecake	276	Sara Lee Cheesecake, lite	150
Croissant	350	Bread, 2 slices	150

Now it's your turn.

Better Choices for My Diet

NEW FOOD	CALORIES	FAT GRAMS	SAVINGS

Go Slowly

Once you have decided on a few easy changes to your diet, like choosing a roast beef sandwich for lunch instead of a Burger King Double Whopper, or eating two slices of whole-wheat toast with peanut butter for breakfast rather than two doughnuts, practice doing this for a few weeks. Don't try to rearrange your entire life all at once.

When you're comfortable with the new changes you've made, move on to the next step. Look over your weekly food records again and see what other foods you might want to eliminate or replace. Maybe you're now ready to try a change you weren't crazy about earlier. If not, what about eating *less* of those hard-to-give-up foods? For example, do you have two Danish pastries each morning? How about just having one, or how about having one every other morning? Do you swing by Starbucks and pick up a Frappuccino Blended Crème? How about ordering it with low-fat milk or nonfat milk?

What about when you eat at home? What can you cut here and still feel satisfied? Start with breakfast: Do you like cereal? What kind of milk do you put on it – whole milk, 2 percent, or 1 percent? You could save up to 100 calories by switching to low-fat or nonfat milk. Do you slather your toast with butter? Could you try a light spread on it, or how about using peanut butter in place of butter? The calories in peanut butter are the same as in butter, but because peanut butter contains protein the combo will keep you going longer, which will make you less tempted to snack. For lunch, do you make your own sandwiches? How much mayonnaise do you use? The calories in mayo are high – the same as butter. Could you be as happy with light mayo, mustard, or a low-cal salad dressing? Condiments add up, so it's good to be aware of how much you're using and how many calories they contain.

Dinner is probably the most unpredictable. Some nights Mom cooks, sometimes Dad, or maybe you go out to a restaurant or grab takeout. When another person in the family prepares or buys the food, it's hard to resist, especially when it tastes so good. But if you find yourself consuming a lot of fried foods, gravies, sauces, and goodies, you might speak up and suggest that on some nights the meals be healthier. Your parents would probably love to help support you with your weight loss, and if you ask them for help, they may be willing to do whatever you want. You can even educate them on the calorie and fat content of foods on your list. This doesn't always work, however, as sometimes family members are resistant to change. If this is the case, let it go and just take smaller portions. You're still ahead.

There are so many ways to trim calories. In the chart below, I've listed additional substitutions you may not have considered.

Ideas for Cutting Calories and Fat

INSTEAD OF...	TRY...
Whole milk or cream	Nonfat or 1 percent milk
Sour cream or mayonnaise	Lite sour cream and lite mayo
Regular cheese	Low-fat cheese
Regular salad dressing	Low-fat dressing or yogurt
Fatty meats (e.g., prime rib)	Lean meats (e.g., flank steak)
Ground beef	Ground turkey
Dark meat (chicken leg)	Light meat (chicken breast)
Poultry with skin	Poultry without skin
Fried or breaded foods	Broiled, roasted, or steamed foods
Cream sauce (Alfredo)	Spaghetti sauce (red)
Butter on pancakes	Fresh fruit on pancakes
Chips, nuts, crackers	Popcorn, pretzels
Doughnuts, pastries	Whole-grain bread
Cookies	Graham crackers
Soda pop	Water flavored with small amount of juice

Eating Healthy Foods Helps Keep the Weight Off

As a nutritionist and a mother, I just can't help putting in a plug for healthy foods. I know I said it is your plan, and I still want the foods you select to be your decision. But I also care about your health and fitness. We now know for sure that many diseases that happen later in life begin with our early eating habits. So to keep you as healthy as possible I want to go over some very basic points about good nutrition. In the long run, these suggestions will enable you to lose weight and keep it off, so it's still relevant to our topic. Besides, you only get one body, so it's very important to respect and care for it.

> **tip** Even moderate nutritional deficiencies will affect school performance.

There are three cardinal rules for good nutrition that I learned in my very first nutrition class. They are variety, balance, and moderation. I would like to explain each briefly and tell you why they are so important not only to your health, but also to your weight loss.

VARIETY

Variety is more than just the spice of life; it is essential to life. Without diversity in foods we may be missing any number of important nutrients needed for growth and development. I mentioned earlier in the chapter that we tend to get in a rut when it comes to food. I remember that my dad would make something like rice pudding and eat it for several months until he got tired of it and moved on to meatloaf. This is NOT a good plan. Of course you can't tell your parents anything, right?

You kept your food record for a week. How many different foods do you eat each week? Do you eat the same thing every day for breakfast, snack, and meals, or do you vary your foods? It's so important that you try to choose different things each day, because by doing so you are more likely to get a full range of nutrients. If you just stick with a few

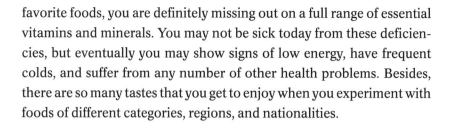

favorite foods, you are definitely missing out on a full range of essential vitamins and minerals. You may not be sick today from these deficiencies, but eventually you may show signs of low energy, have frequent colds, and suffer from any number of other health problems. Besides, there are so many tastes that you get to enjoy when you experiment with foods of different categories, regions, and nationalities.

MODERATION

Overindulgence on a regular basis will prevent you from losing weight. Certainly there are times when we go overboard – Thanksgiving and birthdays come to mind. You would have to be a saint not to indulge in holiday goodies. But we can't do this regularly if we want to shave off some pounds. You will find that the practice of moderation works in many other areas of your life.

BALANCE

All three of these principals have value, but I must say that even diet experts abuse the rule of balance. For optimum health it is vital to choose foods from the three major food groups: protein, carbohydrates, and fats. When you eliminate any one of these groups – as many diet plans do in an attempt to make their program unique – you break a rule and potentially harm your body. When our total being is balanced – our body, mind, and spirit – we seem to live more contently with ourselves and within the world. Likewise, when we balance all three major nutrients within our diet, our bodies function better and we thrive with good health and stable weight.

1. Proteins

Proteins contain the building blocks of life, called amino acids. Amino acids make up our cells, tissues, organs, blood, hormones, and immune systems. Sound important? It is. You find proteins in meats, poultry (chicken and turkey), eggs, fish, nuts, beans, tofu and other soy products, and in dairy foods (milk, yogurt, cheese). Eating some protein at each meal will help to curb your appetite, give you more energy, and help you concentrate better. When I was a student, I always had an egg with toast on the day of a test. Cereal made me sluggish, but the egg helped me be alert even if the test came right before lunch.

It's a good idea to include some sort of protein food with each meal to ward off those out-of-control cravings. Add some protein to your carbohydrate intake in order to keep your blood sugar from spiking. For example, if you have a cookie, balance it with milk. Marie Callender's restaurant has a saying on its pie menu: "A piece of apple pie without cheese is like a kiss without a squeeze." Even I know that's corny, but they have the right idea in recommending protein (cheese) with their pie.

2. Carbohydrates

There seems to be a lot of confusion at this time concerning the role of carbohydrates. So many diets have almost totally eliminated carbs from their plan, and, honestly, I think that is a big mistake – primarily because it neglects the role of balance. By focusing on cutting out carbs, dieters miss essential fruits, vegetables, and whole grains that are necessary for vitamin, mineral, and fiber content. Sure, you control the intake of food, but you can still do that when you include all three major nutrients.

Carbohydrates are fuel for the brain. Without them you feel groggy, moody, and tired. You may become constipated from lack of adequate fiber, and a diet that centers around fat and protein and that bans or limits carbs will often cause gas and bad breath.

What you need to know about carbohydrates is that there are two kinds, and one is better than the other. Simple carbohydrates should be eaten only in limited amounts because they cause your blood sugar to spike very quickly and then to drop just as quickly soon afterward. When this happens, like it does when you eat cookies, cakes, desserts of all kinds, white breads, and French fries, you crave even more sugary foods. It's a vicious cycle. You eat sugar and you crave more. These sugary, white products are usually combined with fats and are stored in the body very easily. Even some of the nonfat snacks are high in fat-storing, simple carbohydrates and should be avoided.

Complex carbohydrates, on the other hand, are digested at an even pace; therefore, they don't cause big surges in blood sugar and are less likely to be stored in the body as fat. They also contain fiber (some more than others), which helps them pass through the system very quickly. The best carbohydrates to include in your menu plan are whole-grain breads and cereals, brown rice, beans, lentils, fruits, and vegetables.

3. Fats

Some popular diets promote cutting out most of the fat in the diet to induce weight loss. There's no doubt the pounds will drop during a drastic reduction in the consumption of fat, but your health will suffer. We need fat in our diets to protect our organs, keep our skin and hair looking healthy, and help us absorb important fat-soluble nutrients. It's a good idea to watch the total amount of fat we take in; however, to eliminate it entirely is a big mistake.

Just like the carbohydrate family of foods, fats are divided into a few groups, some of which are better than others. The ones nutritionists suggest we keep at a minimum are saturated fats and trans fats. Saturated fats are primarily found in meat and dairy products. This is why we keep pushing low-fat milk (as opposed to whole milk), low-fat cheeses, and lite ice cream. To trim even more saturated fat from the diet, remove the excess white fat from meat and the skin from chicken.

Trans fats are front-page news. You may have heard that restaurants like McDonald's are switching from cooking with trans fats to using healthier oils. And manufacturers of all sorts of food products are advertising "no trans fats" on their labels. Trans fats are the worst of all the fats, and they are found in many of the boxed and packaged goodies we buy at the supermarket. If you see the word "hydrogenated" on the ingredients list, the translation is "trans fat," so pick something else.

The goal is to eat more healthy oils, which are found in fish, nuts, seeds, and avocados.

 Never eliminate a major food group from your diet (protein, carbohydrates, or fats).

For a balanced diet, it is good to include all of the following foods in your daily plan. Are there any holes in your diet right now? Guys should shoot for the higher number of servings, girls the lower.

For a Balanced Diet

FOOD GROUP	SERVINGS/DAY
Meat, chicken, fish, nuts, beans, tofu	3–4
Milk and dairy	2–3
Whole-grain breads and cereals, pasta, rice	6–11
Fruits	2–3
Vegetables	3–5

The Basics of Reading Food Labels

A necessary part of your program is to learn how to decipher food labels. Every box, can, bottle, or jar that you have in your cupboard contains certain information on it, some of which you need to be familiar with. The label tells you everything that is in the food. You probably won't be interested in all of the nutritional info provided. But since you are concerned about weight loss, it would be helpful to learn some of the basics; otherwise, you could be eating more calories or fat than you think you are. Let's start at the top of the label, which is usually titled "Nutrition Facts."

SERVING SIZE

Serving size, or portion size, is the first bit of information provided. It can be expressed as a cup, a tablespoon, or some other measurement, depending on the food, and it usually has a metric equivalent next to it as well, like grams (g) or milligrams (mg). Once you start looking at labels, you may be surprised by what a serving size really is. If you inspect some of those small bags of chips that you bought at the convenience store, you will find that they contain two servings. This can be very misleading, I know. If you're going to eat cereal in the morning, check the serving size. The standard serving is 3/4 of a cup, which may not fill your entire bowl. Measure the portion yourself, so you know what 3/4 cup looks like. But don't assume that all cereals use the same amount for a serving size. Some use 1/2 cup (like Grape-Nuts); others use 1 cup (like Cheerios).

CALORIES AND FAT GRAMS

Moving down the label, we come to listings for calories and total fat. There can be great variability in products if you make comparisons. For example, Weight Watchers chicken nuggets contain 180 calories and 11 fat grams, while Banquet chicken nuggets weigh in at 239 calories and 16 fat grams. Breakfast bars can sometimes serve as a quick meal or snack, but read the label before you buy. Planter's Honey Roasted Bar has 230 calories with 13 grams of fat, while Post Raisin Bran Cereal Bar contains 120 calories and 2 grams of fat.

SUGAR

Under the heading "total carbohydrate" you will find a listing for sugars. It is no secret that many of us eat too much sugar overall. Unfortunately, sometimes we don't even realize that we're eating a food or drinking a beverage that is loaded with sugar. Not only does an overdose of sugar prevent you from losing weight, but it also plays havoc with your digestive system and hormonal levels – not to mention cause cavities and sometimes an insatiable need for more sugar. It's very important that we pay attention to food labels and the many forms of hidden sugar.

It's not entirely obvious from the label how much sugar you're getting in relation to other nutrients. However, looking now at the list of ingredients, know that they are listed in order from most to least. In other words, the first ingredient listed is the most plentiful, so the closer sugar comes to the top of the list, the more sugar there is in the product. That's the easy part. The hard part is recognizing all the names for sugar. Some are obvious: brown sugar, honey, syrup, or molasses. Others are not so obvious. Here's a clue: Look for words with "-ose" in them – glucose, sucrose, fructose, lactose, maltose, and dextrose.

When you read the advertising on the front of a box, like Kellogg's Smart Start, you may not be aware of the food's high sugar content because the colorful writing makes the product sound so healthy: "low fat" "vitamins and minerals" "antioxidants" "multi-grain flakes," and "lightly sweetened." It's only when you turn the box on its side and read the ingredients that you count four different kinds of sugar. Sugar itself is listed four times, honey two times, and high-fructose corn syrup (HFCS) two times. Let me list all the different kinds of sugar that are included in the ingredients list on one box of Smart Start cereal: sugar, sugar, sugar, high-fructose corn syrup, molasses, honey, sugar, corn syrup, honey, high-fructose corn syrup, honey. The grand total in a serving is 14 grams of sugar, which equal 3.5 teaspoons. And if you dip into the sugar bowl and add more – well, I'll just say you're getting *way* too much sugar in one meal. Hint: Choose cereals with no more than 8 grams of sugar per serving. For example, plain Cheerios contain 1 gram of sugar per serving. If you want some sweetness, add a banana or some berries instead of dousing it with sugar.

The measurement for sugar is listed on food labels in grams. Most of us cannot relate to how much is in a gram, so I would like you to know how to figure out how many teaspoons you are getting per gram. Then you can find a teaspoon in the kitchen drawer and measure for yourself. To figure out how many teaspoons you're getting from the number of grams of sugar, take the grams per serving and divide by four. It's simple math. For example, a 12-ounce can of soda has 40 grams of sugar. Divide four into forty and you come up with 10 teaspoons of sugar. Depending on how many sodas you drink in a day, this is a potentially *huge* source of sugar in your diet – especially considering the fact that even one soda delivers a tremendous amount of sugar and calories without providing an ounce of nutrition.

> **tip** Total sugar should not exceed 12–18 teaspoons per day.

I want to single out one type of sugar that is prevalent in many products but especially sodas and other drinks, juices, syrups, ketchup, Miracle Whip, and fat-free products. It called high-fructose corn syrup (sometimes listed as HFCS). This man-made form of sugar is not absorbed in the body like real sugar is; instead, it is metabolized into fat in the liver. **HFCS is considered one of the leading causes of overweight and obesity, type-2 diabetes, and other related illnesses.** If a good part of your present diet includes many sodas a day and large amounts of fat-free goodies that contain HFCS, I would strongly recommend that this be something you consider changing for your health as well as for your weight.

MISCELLANEOUS INFORMATION

Labels are highly informative, but I don't want to overwhelm you with more info than you want. You will also see listings for sodium, fiber, protein, and nutritional content. These are all important. If you frequent fast-food establishments and eat a lot of convenience foods each day, you're likely going over the top with your salt or sodium intake. Just be aware that the recommended sodium limit is 2,400 milligrams (mg) per day.

The amount of fiber most Americans get in their diets is abysmally low, so, when you're ready, check out grams of fiber on food labels. If you are eating five or six servings of fruits, vegetables, beans, or whole-grain breads and cereals each day, you are most likely getting close to the recommended 30 grams of fiber.

Help!
What to Eat?
What to Eat?

Now the real work begins. You realize you need to make changes, and I hope that the information I've already provided has helped you spot areas where you can easily shave off calories. However, that may not be enough. You may require additional options. So the next step is to figure out the number of calories and fat grams contained in your meals, snacks, desserts, and drinks so that you can go further in selecting foods that best suit both your tastes and needs. In this chapter I provide information for just a sampling of foods, because as you will see there is wide variability. For more details about calories, check out the websites listed in the Resources section at the back of the book. By consulting these websites you will likely be able to track down the exact food you eat and its caloric value. There are also many books that provide such lists, and by all means, inspect the package labels on the foods in your home.

Breakfast

I know that many of you don't take the time for breakfast, but I want you to reconsider its importance as you are trying to lose weight. There's a heap of research showing that people who skip the first meal of the day keep more fat on their bodies and have a harder time losing weight in general than those who take the time to eat breakfast. If you eat something, especially food with some protein and fiber, like an egg and a whole-grain muffin, you are less likely to snack midmorning and more likely to keep your calories under control all day long.

> ## tip
> **Eating breakfast can boost your metabolic rate by 300 calories.**

It's a common practice among dieters to avoid eating all day and then to gorge at dinner. This habit is not only unhealthy, but it also slows metabolism down during the day so that when you do eat, you will store even more of that meal as fat. If you spread out the same amount of food over the whole day rather than eating it all at once, you are much more likely to lose weight. *FYI: Food eaten earlier in the day is more likely to be burned up for energy and not stored as fat.*

Whether you're eating at home, picking something up at the convenience store, or grabbing a bagel, there are a few tips I would like to suggest as you design your strategy. Balancing your food groups is vital, but it may be most difficult at breakfast. Remember the three major food groups: protein, carbohydrates, and fats? See how you can get all three at breakfast. I know you're thinking, *"I'm lucky if I can wait for the Pop-Tart to spring out of the toaster, and you want me to figure out how I can eat three food groups?"* Really, it's not that difficult if you plan. But first let me tell you why this is so. When you add protein (egg, milk, cheese, yogurt, beans, tofu, meat, or poultry) to a carbohydrate, you blunt the effects of the sugar rush, and this means you will not be as ravenous two hours later. For example, have milk with your breakfast bar, or peanut butter on your toast, or cream cheese on the bagel, or cheese with your Danish.

Watch the excessive use of sugar. If we grab anything at all first thing in the morning it's typically something sweet and gooey with almost no nutritional value, like a doughnut, cinnamon roll, or muffin. Also, we are living in the age of the super-sized meal. No matter where you go, food portions are gigantic. We may not even realize how much sugar and fat we're getting. Pass on the oversized Cinnabon at the mall with its 12 teaspoons of sugar. You might consider cutting down on colas (which each contain 10 teaspoons of sugar) and switching to low-fat milk or fruit juice. And don't even get me started on the once-healthy breakfast cereals. Many of them, especially those with cartoon characters on the front, are made from refined white flour with so much added sugar that it outweighs the nutritional value. If it's sweet, just say no. Buy nonsweetened cereal and add a pinch of sugar – or, better yet, some fresh fruit – yourself.

Condiments are another morning trap. They sneak the pounds on and we barely notice. I'm not saying that you have to totally eliminate butter, syrup, jam, peanut butter, and cream cheese, but you can make a huge difference by spreading less of these on your toast or switching to a lighter version. Butter contains 100 calories per tablespoon, cream cheese is half that at 50 calories per tablespoon, and low-fat cream cheese is half that. If you switched from butter to jam or fruit on your toast (I like banana), you could lose – or avoid gaining – up to fifteen pounds a year.

■ Healthy suggestions for breakfast

Note that I haven't included portion sizes for most items in these lists of healthy meal options. That's because I don't want you to obsess about weighing and measuring your foods. However, as I've said, portion size is a *huge* deal when it comes to losing or maintaining weight. The calorie estimates listed here are for moderate-size portions – not too big, not too skimpy.

✘ Whole-grain cereal with ½ cup of 1 percent milk; banana, berries, or raisins (about 330 calories)

✘ Yogurt with fresh fruit or granola or both (about 300 calories)

✘ Whole-wheat bagel with low-fat cream cheese and an orange or an apple (about 400 calories)

✘ Scrambled eggs with whole-wheat toast and 1 tsp of jam (about 235 calories)

✘ Whole-grain English muffin with 1 Tbsp of peanut butter and an apple, orange, or banana (about 305 calories)

✘ Oatmeal with 1 cup low-fat milk, raisins, or granola (about 355 calories)

I understand that you may not like all of my ideas. Work with the following list to see what you actually do eat and what it costs you.

Breakfast Choices

Note: Whenever you see a specific brand-name food item mentioned in this book, or a specific menu item from a well-known restaurant, be aware that its precise name or caloric content may vary from what is listed here. A food item may be called different things in different parts of the country, or its name may be changed or updated. Caloric and fat content may also vary. If you want the most current information on a particular food, visit the company's or restaurant's website and click on "menu" or "nutritional information."

FOOD	CALORIES	FAT GRAMS
General Mills Cheerios (¾ cup)	110	2
Cheerios with ½ cup 1 percent milk	170	3.5
Kashi Go Lean (1 cup)	140	1
Kellogg's Smart Start (1 cup)	190	1
Quaker Oats (½ cup dry)	150	3
Nature Valley Granola (⅓ cup)	130	6
Gram's Gourmet Granola (½ cup)	349	30
1 egg	75	6

(cont'd.)

Breakfast Choices (cont'd.)

FOOD	CALORIES	FAT GRAMS
Whole-wheat bread	70	1
Post Raisin Bran Cereal Bar	120	2
Power Bar	190	9
Large bagel	280	2
Whole-wheat muffin	130	1
Trail Nut Mix (1½ oz)	230	12
Peanut butter (1 Tbsp)	95	8
Butter or oil (1 Tbsp)	100	11
Sugar (1 Tbsp)	45	0
Jam (1 Tbsp)	50	0
Cream cheese, regular (1 oz or 2 Tbsp)	99	10
Cream cheese, low-fat (1 oz)	50	5
Low-fat yogurt with fruit (8 oz)	225	3
Non-fat yogurt, plain (8 oz)	127	Trace
Stick of skim mozzarella cheese (string cheese)	70	4
Banana	90	0
Orange	80	0
Strawberries (1 cup)	45	0
Raisins (2 Tbsp)	85	0

(cont'd.)

Breakfast Choices (cont'd.)

FOOD	CALORIES	FAT GRAMS
Fast Food		
McDonald's Deluxe Breakfast	1,190	61
McDonald's Hotcakes and Sausage	780	33
McDonald's Biscuits w/Sausage and Eggs	520	34
McDonald's Egg McMuffin	300	12
McDonald's Scrambled Eggs	160	11
McDonald's Apple Bran Muffin	190	0
Carl's Jr. Low Carb Breakfast Bowl	900	73
Carl's Jr. Breakfast Quesadilla	391	18
Carl's Jr. Scrambled Eggs	180	14
Carl's Jr. English Muffin w/margarine	206	9
Burger King Scrambled Eggs Breakfast Sausage	900	57
Burger King Bagel with Cream Cheese	370	16
Burger King French Toast Sticks	390	20
Dunkin' Donuts Coffee Cake Muffin w/ Topping	710	29
Dunkin' Donuts Bagel Egg Sausage Cheese Sandwich	670	28
Dunkin' Donuts Plain Bagel	360	3
Dunkin' Donuts Glazed Doughnut	180	8

(cont'd.)

Breakfast Choices (cont'd.)

FOOD	CALORIES	FAT GRAMS
Krispy Kreme Apple Fritter	380	21
Krispy Kreme Chocolate Iced Cake Doughnut	270	14
Krispy Kreme Original Glazed Doughnut	200	12

Lunch

Lunch may be a greater challenge in a different way. More often than not you are away from home and your choices are limited, especially if you eat in the school cafeteria. If you can make your own lunch, you have more flexibility and control. If you stop by the local market, deli, or fast-food restaurant with little time, you tend to select what's quickest. Eating with friends often influences what you eat for lunch. Maybe you don't want them to know you're trying to lose weight. Possibly you eat very little because you want your friends to see that you really don't eat that much and then, by mid-afternoon, you're ready to inhale the first morsel you can lay your hands on. I urge you not to skip lunch and also to think about choosing foods that will provide you with the energy you need to keep you going throughout the day.

> **tip** Eat slowly—it takes twenty minutes for your brain to register that your stomach is full.

Just a few pointers before you examine the lunch list. Watch out for the extra cheese. Sandwiches and hamburgers—everything seems to come slathered in cheese. It's not that cheese isn't a good choice sometimes. It can be a great source of calcium and protein. Unfortunately, the fat it contains makes it one of those items we need to limit. Most cheese averages about 100 calories per ounce (2 tablespoons). Leave it off or look for the low-fat and light brands. Low-fat cheeses slice half the calories off the regular version. Sometimes the server at a restaurant adds cheese even when you ask them not to. In this case, scrape off what you can. You get to enjoy the flavor without all the calories.

Fried foods are not the healthiest choices. Any time you can cut down on them or substitute something else it shows that you are working your plan and caring for your body. Small changes can make a big difference. For example, if you switched from the large fries at 500 calories to the smaller order at 230, you could save 270 calories each time. Let's say you did this three times a week for a year. You would lose, or avoid gaining, eleven pounds.

It's the little things that increase our waist and thighs inch by inch. Things like salad dressings and dips can ruin a healthy meal. At McDonald's you can select a healthy grilled-chicken salad that contains 270 calories, but if you smother it in ranch dressing at 290 calories a dollop, you've more than doubled the caloric count. If ranch is your favorite, try using less, even half. If you are up for trying something different, go for the low-fat vinaigrette at 40 calories a packet.

Size always matters when it comes to food. Bigger is NOT better. Schlotzsky's Deli has an Original Turkey Sandwich that weighs in at 17 ounces for a whopping 1,020 calories and 51 grams of fat (way more than any gal or guy needs). Schlotzsky's also offers a Light and Flavorful Smoked Turkey Sandwich that weighs 13 ounces and comes in at 500 calories and 7 fat grams. We're talking one-half the calories and one-seventh the fat grams.

Comparison shopping definitely pays off. We tend to think that chicken is always better than beef, but that's not necessarily the case. Carl's Jr. serves a healthy-sounding Charbroiled Chicken Club Sandwich containing 510 calories, while its Happy Star Hamburger (my favorite) contains only 330 calories.

A lunch favorite for dieters is soup. Once again, there's great variety in the calories and fat contained in soups. Cream soups offer more of both – often a significant amount more. Au Bon Pain prepares a potato cheese soup containing 190 calories, but you could slash more calories by ordering the chicken noodle at 100 calories a serving. Chili is generally a good lunch selection and it often comes with turkey or without meat at all. Sometimes even a small order of chili can be very filling.

Again, I ask that you consider balancing your food groups to include a protein, complex carbohydrate, fruit and/or vegetable. There is variability in foods you find at restaurants, so what you select may not have exactly the same number of calories and fat grams as the ones in the lists that follow. That's fine. These numbers are to be used as tools for making wise choices. I don't want you to feel you have to be obsessive about every little calorie or gram of fat.

■ Examples of healthy lunches

- ✗ Turkey sandwich on whole-wheat bread with lettuce, tomato, and mustard; fruit (about 400 calories)
- ✗ Chicken breast on bun with lettuce, tomato, low-fat salad dressing; fruit (about 300 calories)
- ✗ Salad bar (lettuce, various veggies, seeds, shrimp or egg), low-fat dressing; four crackers (about 300 calories)
- ✗ Ham & Swiss cheese on rye bread with mustard; fruit salad, water-packed (about 480 calories)
- ✗ Vegetable pizza (6 oz slice); green salad with low-fat dressing (about 500 calories)
- ✗ Soup – vegetable beef, split pea, chicken vegetable, lentil; whole-grain roll; fruit (about 250 calories)
- ✗ 2 soft tacos (chicken, beef, or fish) with lettuce, tomato, salsa; fruit (about 250 calories)
- ✗ Peanut butter and jelly sandwich on whole-wheat bread; fruit (about 420 calories)

✗ Turkey or veggie burger with bun, lettuce, tomato, mustard; fruit (about 400 calories)

✗ Denny's vegetable cheese omelet – eggs, mushrooms, green pepper, onion, salsa on the side; apple sauce (about 574 calories)

✗ Chili; cornbread; fruit (about 500 calories)

✗ Small burrito; fruit (about 500 calories)

I hope you're picking up some healthy hints. Now for some fast-food choices.

Fast-Food Choices

FOOD	CALORIES	FAT GRAMS
Au Bon Pain		
Soup Bread Bowl (9.25 oz)	600	3
Potato Cheese Soup (8 oz)	190	10
Vegetarian Chili (8 oz)	170	2
Vegetable Beef Barley Soup (8 oz)	110	3
Chicken Noodle Soup (8 oz)	100	2
Bagel Cinnamon Crisp	540	7
Muffin, Carrot	520	25
Cookie, Peanut Butter (2 oz)	240	12
Cookie, Chocolate Chip (2 oz)	230	7
Bread Stick	200	3
Baja Fresh		
Burrito, Bean & Cheese Chicken	1,000	33

(cont'd.)

Fast-Food Choices (cont'd.)

FOOD	CALORIES	FAT GRAMS
Burrito Ultimo Chicken	860	30
Taquitos, Chicken with Bean	710	36
Taco, Chilito Steak	340	10
Taco, Baja Style Chicken	190	5
Subway		
Subway Meat & Italian BMT (6 inch)	630	35
Subway Chicken Fajita	510	21
Subway Meatloaf (6 inch)	501	25
Subway Melt	384	15
Subway Gardenburger	370	7
Subway Chicken Breast	291	5
Subway Roast Beef, regular	267	5
Fruizle Smoothie, small	221	1
Mayonnaise (1 Tbsp)	111	12
Mayonnaise, light (1 Tbsp)	46	5
Mustard (2 tsp)	7	0
Provolone circles, 2 halves	51	4
El Pollo Loco		
Tostada Salad	700	32
Buttermilk Ranch Dressing (3 Tbsp)	220	24

(cont'd.)

Fast-Food Choices (cont'd.)

FOOD	CALORIES	FAT GRAMS
Light Italian Dressing (3 Tbsp)	20	0
Salsa (3 Tbsp)	9	Trace
Ultimate Chicken Burrito	685	23
Chicken Lover's Burrito	525	18
Taco, Soft Chicken (1)	237	12
Schlotzsky's Deli		
Sandwich, Original Turkey (17 oz)	1,020	51
Pastrami Reuben (16 oz)	920	43
Specialty Deli LT (10 oz)	580	24
Light and Flavorful Smoked Turkey (13 oz)	500	7
Sbarro		
Baked Ziti (14 oz)	830	42
Meat Lasagna (17 oz)	730	38
Spaghetti with Sauce (18 oz)	630	18
Pizza, Sausage & Pepperoni Stuffed (11 oz)	880	44
Pizza, Pepperoni (1 serving)	510	21
Pizza, Cheese	450	14
Pizza Hut		
Pan Meat Lovers (1 medium slice)	340	19
Hand Tossed Pepperoni (1 med slice)	250	9

(cont'd.)

Fast-Food Choices (cont'd.)

FOOD	CALORIES	FAT GRAMS
Thin 'N Crispy Cheese (1 med slice)	200	8
Fit 'N Delicious (1 med slice)	160	5
Hot Wings (2 pieces)	110	6
Blue Cheese Dipping Sauce (1 serving)	220	23
Burger King		
Classic Coke (small)	160	0
Classic Coke (large)	330	0
Chocolate Shake (small)	620	32
Double Whopper with Cheese	1,070	70
Double Cheeseburger	540	31
Grilled Chicken Sandwich	540	27
Hamburger	310	14
French Fries (small)	230	11
French Fries (large)	500	25
Salad, Chicken Caesar without dressing	230	7
Dressing, Creamy Caesar (1 serving)	140	13
McDonald's		
Double Quarter Pounder with Cheese	760	48
Big Mac	560	33

(cont'd.)

Fast-Food Choices (cont'd.)

FOOD	CALORIES	FAT GRAMS
Double Cheeseburger	480	27
Chicken McGrill	400	17
Chicken McNuggets (6 pieces)	310	20
Salad, Crispy Chicken California Cobb	380	22
Dressing, Newman's Own Cobb (1 serving)	120	9
Salad, Grilled Chicken Ranch	270	13
Dressing, Newman's Ranch	290	30
Dressing, Newman's Low-Fat Vinaigrette	40	0
Wendy's		
Big Bacon Classic	580	30
Classic Single with Everything	410	19
Chili, large (12 oz)	310	10
Chili, small (8 oz)	210	7
Potato, Baked, Plain	310	0
Potato, Baked, Bacon & Cheese	530	18
Chicken Nuggets (5 piece)	230	16
Nuggets Honey Mustard Sauce	130	12
Nuggets Barbecue Sauce	45	0

Dinner

Dinner is unique in that it may be the one meal of the day where you get to spend time with your family. It may be the one meal that is prepared and placed in front of you to enjoy. It may also be the one meal about which you have little to no choice. If you're lucky, your mom, dad, or whoever does the cooking in your family will ask you for your ideas or preferences and you can talk to them about the recommendations in this book. Hopefully, they will be very supportive and open to trying new recipes.

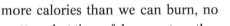

The last meal of the day usually involves the most food. I think it would be healthier if we were to spread our calories out more evenly so that no one meal is outrageously large. Whenever we consume more calories than we can burn, no matter what time of day, we store the extra calories as fat.

How healthy your dinner is and whether it helps you to gain or maintain your weight depends on your family's heritage and style of cooking. Your mom may have learned how to make wonderful fried chicken from your grandmother, and she may love to cook up vegetables swimming in gravy or pot roast with mashed potatoes and biscuits, not to mention the homemade pies. Once you have a taste for these foods, it's hard to resist them because they remind you of pleasant times around the dinner table. And let's face it, they also taste fantastic. Fat has the most flavor of all the food groups. No wonder we like it. However, if you want to lose weight, you may have to make some adjustments at dinner as well. You can ask your parent or caregiver to help prepare lower-fat foods, but if that is not their thing, then you need to adjust by taking smaller portions. Actually, you can escape many of those fatty calories by scraping some of the breading off the chicken, pouring less gravy on your potatoes, and passing on the biscuits. You'll still get a hint of the flavor.

I'm not providing you with a list of dinner suggestions because I don't know what you like to eat and the possibilities are limitless. Therefore, I'm going to offer options of frozen dinners that you could make for yourself if no one is available to cook, as well as samples of dinners you can order at various restaurants. These may not have exactly the same calories as your entree at home, but you will develop an understanding of the caloric content of typical foods.

I hope you remember to include vegetables with your meats and starches to maintain a healthy balance. Vegetables are very low in calories and are not something you should cut from your diet even if you are trying to lose weight. One cup of broccoli or green beans or zucchini contains only 40 calories and no fat grams. Peas, corn, and potatoes have more calories but are still healthy choices. Eat up. Just don't smother your veggies in sauce or butter. Generally, the simpler the preparation, the lower the calories.

Dinner Choices

FOOD	CALORIES	FAT GRAMS
Banquet Frozen Dinners		
Boneless White-Meat Fried Chicken	540	34
Salisbury Steak with Vegetables	318	12
Chicken Parmigiana	320	18
Grilled Chicken	330	18
Meatloaf	280	16
Healthy Choice Frozen Dinners		
Beef Stroganoff	320	8
Beef Teriyaki	310	7

(cont'd.)

Dinner Choices (cont'd.)

FOOD	CALORIES	FAT GRAMS
Chicken Teriyaki with Rice (bowl)	270	4
Tuna Casserole	240	5
Grilled Chicken with Mashed Potato	180	4
Marie Callender's		
Breaded Chicken Parmigiana	860	32
Beef Stroganoff with Noodles	600	27
Breaded Fish with Mac & Cheese	550	28
Beef Pot Roast & Gravy	500	17
Chicken & Dumplings	390	20
Grilled Chicken Breast & Rice Pilaf	360	14
Skillet Meal, Roasted Chicken & Vegetables	260	6
Boston Market		
Chicken Pot Pie	780	46
½ Chicken with Skin	590	33
½ Chicken, No Skin	170	4
Open Face Turkey Sandwich	500	12
Boston Hearth Lean Ham	210	9
Meat Loaf & Brown Gravy	390	22
Potato Salad (¾ cup)	340	24
Cole Slaw (¾ cup)	300	19

(cont'd.)

Dinner Choices (cont'd.)

FOOD	CALORIES	FAT GRAMS
Honey Glazed Carrots (¾ cup)	280	15
Macaroni & Cheese (¾ cup)	280	11
Baked Beans (¾ cup)	270	5
Hot Cinnamon Apples (¾ cup)	250	5
Broccoli Cauliflower au Gratin (¾ cup)	200	11
Broccoli with Red Peppers (¾ cup)	60	4
Mashed Potatoes (⅔ cup)	190	9
Green Bean Casserole (¾ cup)	130	9
Green Beans (¾ cup)	80	6
Corn Bread, 1 serving	200	6
Fruit Salad (¾ cup)	70	1
Steamed Vegetables (⅔ cup)	35	1
Denny's		
Fish & Chips Dinner	955	57
Burger BBQ	953	52
Boca Burger	601	27
T-Bone Steak Dinner	860	65
Sirloin Steak Dinner	337	28
Roast Turkey & Stuffing with Gravy	388	3
Fried Shrimp & Scampi Dinner	346	20

(cont'd.)

Dinner Choices (cont'd.)

FOOD	CALORIES	FAT GRAMS
Soup, Cream of Broccoli	574	43
Soup, Vegetable Beef	79	1
Panda Express		
Spicy Chicken with Peanuts (5 oz)	510	29
Vegetable Fried Rice (8 oz)	410	19
Sweet & Sour Pork (4 oz)	310	13
Orange Chicken (5 oz)	310	13
Steamed Rice (8 oz)	220	0
Beef & Broccoli (5 oz)	180	9
Chicken with String Beans (5 oz)	180	9
Egg Rolls, 2 (3 oz)	190	6
Red Lobster		
Light House Salmon	578	31
Light House King Crab Legs	490	9
Light House Tilapia	346	10
Light House Broiled Flounder	240	5
Light House Maine Lobster Tail	104	5
Fresh Buttered Vegetables	143	12
Fresh Broccoli	60	0

Snacks and Desserts

Snacking is actually good for weight control. You can learn to manage your hunger by eating between meals. Snacks can help to keep your blood-sugar level stable and prevent you from gorging at the next meal. And choosing nutritious snacks is a clever way to sneak in extra nutrients. That's the good news. The bad news is that sometimes eating between meals can spin out of control. If you are munching mindlessly while watching TV, or if you are eating out of boredom, anger, or frustration, you can easily squash your dieting efforts. If you're nodding your head right now, check out the section on emotional eating (Chapter 4) and see what you can do to avoid overeating during these times.

> **tip** One appetizer of fried mozzarella costs 830 calories.

The trick to making snacks work for you is to schedule your food for the following day, including your snacks. When do you normally pick up a little extra something? What do you usually select? Does it still work within your plan? Would another choice be better? Is it something you can buy in advance or prepack at home? Are you planning to stop at 7-Eleven or feed the vending machine? It's best and cheapest if you can make a list of the foods that you like and that travel well. Portion them out in advance and keep them close by, in your car or backpack. For example, fruits are great because they are both convenient and readily available. Apples now come peeled and cut up in small packages. They can be a great sweet treat that costs only 80 calories – that is, unless you dip them in the accompanying caramel syrup, which more than doubles the calories. Nuts are a healthy and filling snack if you don't overdo it. Many also come in convenient sizes. You can get a large bag of natural, nonroasted nuts at Trader Joe's and divide them into individual portions at home.

Breakfast bars make an appealing meal or snack. They're portable, convenient, and individually wrapped. Unfortunately you can't always tell if you're buying a health food or a junk food. You have to do your homework and read the labels. Hint: Check for sugar content.

Tons of snacks are available in convenience sizes – cookies, bars, cheese, yogurt, crackers and peanut butter, puddings, and applesauce. Buying prepackaged individual servings makes it easier if you're one of those people who struggle with polishing off every last crumb. When you have a large bag of chips and you're home alone with nothing to do, it's hard not to nibble through the whole bag before you know it. There's something psychological about completing a task, even when it comes to eating. Anyway, if you first portion out your chips or cookies or just buy small bags, you can eat your way through them and not feel guilty.

Here's something to consider: Are you one of those people for whom a taste of sugar is not enough? Are you not satisfied with one or two cookies, and you inevitably eat ten? If this is the case, maybe snacking, at least snacking on sweets, is not for you. Try fruit or cheese or nuts, and see if you get the same response. Nibbling may not be for everyone. If it's easier for you to eat three meals a day and skip the snacks, fine. Just don't skip any meals. I'm one of those for whom snacking on certain foods doesn't work. I don't feel well if I have a midmorning coffee or a midday chocolate. It upsets my stomach and makes my heart race. But after lunch or dinner, bring on the dessert and I won't turn it down. In fact, the meal for me is not complete without a little something sweet. You have to pay attention to what works for you. Listen to your body.

The table below lists snacks that contain less than 100 calories. The table after that shows other snacks, for comparison. I'm not giving you a list of "approved" and "not approved" snacks; you know the "good" snacks and the "bad" snacks. I *am* hoping that from time to time you will try snacks like cut-up carrots and celery, tangerines, and yogurt, because they do carry more nutrients and they do have fewer calories and less fat – but let's be honest, there are times when chocolate chip ice cream is calling our name.

Snacks under 100 Calories

FOOD	CALORIES
Strawberries (1 cup)	45
Apple (1 med)	90
Orange (1 med)	75
Banana (1 small)	100
Grapes (20)	70
Watermelon (½-inch slice)	60
Carrot (1)	30
Baked potato (1 small)	100
Yogurt (4 oz)	60
Yoplait soft frozen-yogurt bar	90
Graham cracker (1 whole)	50
Chocolate chip cookie (1)	100
Sugar wafer (1)	25
Bagel (½)	80
Whole-wheat bread (1 slice)	75
Corn tortilla (6 inch)	65
Flour tortilla (6 inch)	85
English muffin (½)	75
Saltine crackers (5)	60

(cont'd.)

Snacks under 100 Calories (cont'd.)

FOOD	CALORIES
Triscuits (3)	60
Wheat Thins (8)	80
Egg, boiled (1)	90
Popcorn (1 cup air-popped)	25
Minute Maid Fruit Juice (1)	60
Jell-O Pudding Pops (1)	80
Applesauce (½ cup, unsweetened)	52
Cottage cheese, 1 percent (½ cup)	82

Snacks and desserts are often interchangeable. I usually think of a snack as something healthier, like fruit and cheese, and I think of dessert as pie, cake, or ice cream, but the rules are not written in stone. There was a time when I would never have considered fruit a dessert. Now I'm okay with it. And, actually, I have grown to like something light like mangoes, papayas, and tangerines to complete my meal – not every time, but sometimes. Here is your comparison list of various snacks and desserts.

Snacks and Desserts

FOOD	CALORIES	FAT GRAMS
Nuts		
Peanuts/almonds (1 oz or 2 Tbsp)	167	15
Walnuts (1 oz)	182	18

(cont'd.)

Snacks and Deserts (cont'd.)

FOOD	CALORIES	FAT GRAMS
Cashews (1 oz)	163	14
Golden Orchards Pistachios (3 oz package)	240	20
Trail mix (1½ oz)	230	12
Peanut butter (2 Tbsp)	190	17
Bars		
Balance Bar Honey Peanut	310	10
Kashi Go Lean Mocha Java	290	6
Power Bar, chocolate	230	2
Jennie Craig Meal Bar	220	5
Balance Bar, original	200	6
Slim-Fast Peanut Caramel	120	4
Crackers		
Cheez-It Party Mix (½ cup)	140	5
Keebler Paks, Cheese & Peanut Butter (1 package)	190	9
Pepperidge Farm Goldfish on the Go (1 package)	170	7
Cheese cracker with peanut butter filling (1)	34	2
Wheat Thins (7)	67	3
Saltines (5)	70	2
Breton Multi Grain Original (3)	60	3

(cont'd.)

Snacks and Deserts (cont'd.)

FOOD	CALORIES	FAT GRAMS
Popcorn		
Caramel coated (1 cup)	152	5
Chocolate covered (1 cup)	130	5
Air-popped (1 cup)	31	0
Chips		
Lay's Classic Potato Chips (20 chips)	150	10
Tortilla chips (1 oz)	142	7
Corn chips (1 oz)	153	10
Light potato chips (1 oz)	134	6
Lay's Classic Baked Original (11 chips)	110	2
Candy		
Snickers (2.07 oz)	280	14
Butterfinger (2.1 oz)	270	11
M&M's Plain (1 package)	240	10
Planter's Original Peanut Bar (1.6 oz)	230	14
Godiva Chocolate (1.5 oz)	230	130
KitKat Bar (0.6 oz)	80	4
Fudge with nuts (0.7 oz)	80	3
Junior Mints, snack size	75	1
Taffy (1)	56	0

(cont'd.)

Snacks and Deserts (cont'd.)

FOOD	CALORIES	FAT GRAMS
Jelly beans (10 small)	40	0
Hershey's Kisses (1)	25	2
Twizzlers, cherry (1)	30	0
Cookies		
Burger King Fresh Baked Cookie	440	21
Starbucks Oatmeal Raisin	390	15
McDonaldland Cookie	230	8
Mrs. Field's Semi Sweet Chocolate	220	10
Mrs. Field's Peanut Butter	220	12
Mrs. Field's Oatmeal	180	7
SnackWells, Cream Sandwich (package)	210	5
Nabisco Chips Ahoy (3)	170	8
Nabisco Oreo (3)	160	7
Nabisco Oreo Reduced Fat (3)	130	4
Nabisco Animal Crackers (package)	120	3
Cakes		
Boston Market Caramel Pecan Brownie	900	47
Boston Market Chocolate Cake	650	32
Starbucks Hazelnut Coffee Cake	630	35
Starbucks Crumble Berry Coffee Cake	520	26

(cont'd.)

Snacks and Deserts (cont'd.)

FOOD	CALORIES	FAT GRAMS
Starbucks Zucchini Pound Cake	370	19
Sara Lee Cheesecake, French	350	5
Jack-in-the-Box Cheesecake	320	16
Mrs. Field's Carrot Cake	280	13
KFC Fudge Brownie	270	9
Gingerbread	264	12
Desserts		
Tiramisu	409	30
Marie Callender's Apple Cobbler	370	20
Cream puff with chocolate icing and custard filling	336	20
Chocolate cream pie (1 piece)	344	22
Éclair with chocolate icing and custard filling	205	10
Coconut cream pie	191	11
Ice Cream		
Dairy Queen Chocolate Malt, regular	760	18
McDonald's Hot Fudge Sundae	340	12
Drumstick	340	20
Häagen-Dazs Chocolate Chip (½ cup)	300	20

(cont'd.)

Snacks and Deserts (cont'd.)

FOOD	CALORIES	FAT GRAMS
Klondike Bar Crunch	280	20
Dairy Queen Soft Ice Cream Cone, regular	240	7
Healthy Choice Cookies 'N Cream (½ cup)	120	2
Fudgsicle Pop	60	5
Ices/Sherbets		
Häagen-Dazs Sherbet (½ cup)	130	0
Carnation Orange Sherbet (3 oz)	90	1
Fruit and juice bars	75	Trace

Drinks

Liquid calories count. And while drinks are stimulating, soothing, comforting, and refreshing, they are a major source of hidden calories. One drink can shoot your fat grams and sugar quota for the entire day. An iced white-chocolate mocha from Starbucks – a grande with whipped cream and whole milk (don't any of these drinks have shorter names?) – costs you 490 calories, with 210 of those coming from fat, which is more than a McDonald's double cheeseburger. If you cut this one drink out of your diet (assuming you indulge in two a week), you could lose more than a pound a month or thirteen pounds a year. The good news is you have many choices of drinks available that don't put you over the top calorie-wise.

 tip Even mild dehydration can slow your metabolism by as much as 3 percent.

Don't let some of the healthy-sounding names fool you into thinking that your drink is nutritious. Starbucks Blackberry Green Tea Blended Crème contains 560 calories and 9 fat grams. But here's the kicker – it has 78 grams of sugar. Translation: 19.5 teaspoons in one serving.

Let's start with a favorite pastime: stopping off at Starbucks before school to grab a shot of caffeine, or meeting friends there on the weekend for a little latté and light conversation. Coffee, once a zero-calorie beverage, has evolved into an array of flavors and mixers, including whole-milk and nonfat versions, whipped cream, mochas, frappuccinos, macchiatos, and smoothies. It makes the head spin just to read the menu. Here are a few favorites. You can decide if they're worth the calories.

Starbucks Beverages

FLAVOR	CALORIES	FAT GRAMS
Frappuccino, Blended Creme	560	10
Frappuccino, Caramel or Mocha	430	10
Frappuccino Light, Caramel or Mocha	180	0
Frappuccino, Coffee, No Cream	260	2
Latte, Eggnog, Whipped Cream, Grande with Whole Milk	510	29
Latte, Vanilla (or other flavors), Whole Milk	320	7
Latte, Vanilla (or other flavors), Nonfat Milk	230	0
Latte, Chai Tea Latte, Nonfat Milk	230	0

(cont'd.)

Starbucks Beverages (cont'd.)

FLAVOR	CALORIES	FAT GRAMS
Caffe Latte, Nonfat	160	0
Macchiato, Caramel, Whole Milk	310	7
Macchiato, Caramel, Nonfat Milk	220	1
Macchiato, Iced Caramel Soy (Tall)	160	1
Cappuccino, Whole Milk	150	5
Cappuccino, Soy Milk	120	0
Hot Chocolate, Whole Milk	450	14
Hot Chocolate, Nonfat Milk	210	0
Apple Juice, Grande	230	0
Green, Black, or Passion Iced Tea	80	0
Caffe Americano	20	0
Coffee, regular or decaf	10	0
Espresso (2 oz)	10	0

SODAS

I know this is your diet and I said I wouldn't try to *make* you change anything, but if I could, it would be to get you to stop drinking sodas or at least to cut down on the number of sodas you drink. Not only are carbonated beverages a huge source of calories; they are really bad for your body. They are made up of sugar, water, and a bunch of not-so-healthy additives. The type of sugar that is used to sweeten soda is what bothers me the most. It's a very inexpensive type of sugar called high-fructose corn syrup (HFCS), and it is added to thousands of other products as well. Just check out the labels in the cupboard at home or at the market and see for yourself how many times you find HFCS listed on soda and many other products.

There are so many reasons why HFCS should be avoided, but the one that may interest you the most is that it causes fat to be stored easily in the body, thus contributing to weight gain. For some reason this liquid sugar is digested differently than regular table sugar, increasing blood fats and putting you at risk for type-2 diabetes and other weight-related illnesses. In addition, carbonated beverages are very acidic and often cause indigestion as well as weakened bones. A study published in the *American Journal of Clinical Nutrition* (2006) found that drinking just three colas a week (including diet colas) may lower hipbone density in women. You may not care about your bones today, but the type of bone you build now will affect you in later years when it's too late to reverse the process.

tip Drinking one can of soda each day can cause you to put on fifteen pounds a year.

Drinking sodas daily replaces other healthy drinks. Twenty years ago teens drank twice as much milk as they did soda, and today the trend has reversed. Most of you are drinking twice as much soda as milk. Not getting adequate calcium may be part of the reason why young people often have fragile bones.

Here are some suggestions:

1. Cut down on any food in which HFCS is listed as one of the first three ingredients.

    To give up one twenty-ounce cola a day would mean losing about half a pound a week, more than two pounds a month, or thirty pounds a year. *FYI: That twenty-ounce soda has sixteen teaspoons of sugar, more than you need in one day (a maximum of thirteen is recommended by the experts).*

2. Go for a smaller size (this is a good pointer for all flavored beverages – not just sodas). You cut calories (and fat grams, in the case of fancy coffee drinks) almost in half by ordering the small or regular size. I know that the larger one is a better buy, but think of your waist rather than your waste.

3. Replace the soda with something that has nutritional value – or at least that doesn't pack on the calories – like low-fat milk, water, plain iced tea, juice, or sparkling water.

Carbonated Beverages

TYPE	CALORIES
Cola (20 oz)	310
Cola (12 oz)	151
Diet Cola	2
Orange soda (12 oz)	177
Root beer (12 oz)	170
Grape soda (12 oz)	161
7-Up (12 oz)	140
Ginger ale (12 oz)	124

DIET SODAS

So you're ready to switch to diet sodas? I hate to be the bearer of doom, but in the case of sodas, sugar-free versions may not be any healthier that sugar-filled ones. First and foremost, the sweetener in diet drinks, aspartame (also known as NutraSweet, Equal, and Spoonful), makes some people crave carbohydrates. This means you cut back on drinking regular sodas only to pick up the calories somewhere else. *FYI: The latest research is finding that the more you use artificial sweeteners, the more likely you are to gain weight.* And if that's not enough, there is a long history of health problems and symptoms in some people who go for diet drinks, including dizziness, headaches, ringing in the ears, anxiety, depression, slurred speech, joint pain, numb legs, or blurred vision. If you've noticed anything like this, definitely stop consuming any drinks that contain aspartame. Some researchers have found that aspartame may trigger behavior problems in sensitive people. Not everyone is affected like this, but it can be frightening if you are.

I read an article in the December 2006 issue of *Nutrition and Healing Newsletter* that scared me concerning the potential toxicity of this substance. Dr. Jonathon Wright writes about wanting to get rid of some carpenter ants that were eating a small building on his property. Not the type who resorts to poisonous chemicals, he had heard that aspartame had worked for others in a similar situation. You can find aspartame, or Equal, at any restaurant. It's the small blue packet of sugar substitute that is usually located right next to the salt and pepper. By the way, it did kill the ants within a day. This is a tip I'm sure you didn't expect, but it may be useful in the future. Until then, I think I'll take my chances with sugar, in limited amounts, of course.

▦ ENERGY DRINKS

Energy drinks promise to stimulate metabolism, promote weight loss, and boost your energy and endurance. Products like Red Bull, Rockstar, and Monster offer liquid elixirs that are packed with sugar, caffeine, herbs, and megadoses of B-vitamins. They sound almost healthy, and we want to believe that one small can will fulfill all these promises. Unfortunately there is no evidence that the products live up to their claims.

What marketers don't tell you about the energy drinks is that the amount of caffeine in these little containers is two to four times what you would find in a regular cola. The caffeine mixed with sugar gives you that quick sugar jolt, which is followed by an equally fast and unhealthy crash. New research shows that the combination of sugar and caffeine blunts the effect of fat metabolism and causes the body to convert the sugar more rapidly to fat than noncaffeinated soft drinks. Caffeine is a drug to be used with caution. While a small amount of caffeine has positive effects on the body and mind, too much will cause a racing heart, increase your blood pressure, trigger feelings of anxiety, and result in dehydration. Have you ever noticed how thirsty you are after eating too much sugar or drinking too much coffee? This means you're dehydrated.

Energy drinks are not regulated by the federal government and are not something I would recommend, either to help you lose weight or to make you more alert. Increasingly, kids are calling their doctors after getting sick from a caffeine overdose. Maybe we should follow the lead of some European countries like France, Norway, Sweden, and Denmark, which have banned certain energy drinks because of their high levels of caffeine.

SPORTS DRINKS

There is a long aisle at the supermarket packed with sports drinks, so I'm guessing they're a pretty hot item. If you've ever been at the starting line of a marathon or a 10K race, you've probably spotted runners carrying little bottles of various drinks tucked into their pockets. On TV, football stars advertise how a particular drink rehydrates and refuels them for grueling hours on the field. But do YOU need this type of drink when you exercise thirty minutes, three times a week? The answer is no. Unless you are a Peyton Manning out for an intensive workout, or Venus and Serena Williams competing to win a tennis match, you would be better off drinking a cool glass of water. Most of the fitness or vitamin waters are made from sugar, artificial flavors, and a mixture of vitamins and minerals. Some add electrolytes, which you may want to replace if you sweat for several hours. However, if you just perspire from walking briskly through the mall, you would do fine by grabbing a glass of water (to rehydrate you) or eating any fruit or vegetable (to replace electrolytes).

Some of the fitness drinks taste pretty good, and they come in such cool bottles. You are drawn to them. But again, I ask you to inspect the side label and make sure you know what you're drinking. The label on the front that catches your attention can be misleading. I conducted my own research and went to the market to compare waters. I noticed the colorfully packaged line of Glaceau VitaminWaters with impressive names like Energy, Revive, Balance, and Power-C, so I turned a bottle over and read the nutrition facts. In an eight-fluid-ounce portion, you get 40 to 50 calories – better than soda. The added vitamins aren't in megadoses, so I have no problem with that. Then I noticed the serving size: 2.5 servings per container. That I did not expect. You're supposed to share that bottle with one and a half other people? I don't think so. When you do the simple multiplication, it means you're actually drinking 120–150 calories if you down the entire bottle. Even more surprising to me was the amount of sugar, which totaled 32.5 grams (that's 13 grams per 2.5 servings) – almost as much as you would get in a regular cola.

FRUIT JUICE AND FRUIT DRINKS

There is no question that a glass of fresh orange juice is packed with vitamins, minerals, and fiber and is a good choice for any meal or snack. Real fruit juice comes in a variety of preparations. You can get it fresh (which is the best but is not always available), or you can get a pasteurized product in a bottle – not quite as flavorful as fresh-squeezed, but more convenient. Actually that's a matter of taste – my kids prefer the not-so-fresh version. And there is reconstituted juice, made from frozen concentrate. It's the cheapest kind, but it is still acceptable. There are many juices to choose from, all of which offer different nutrients. Calorie levels in fruit juices are generally reasonable. Well, that may not always be true. Look over the following list and see if you can find the fruit drinks you like.

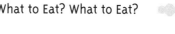

Fruit Juices and Fruit Drinks

BEVERAGE	CALORIES
Jamba Juice, Power Boost (16 oz)	325
Jamba Juice, Lemonade (16 oz)	286
Orange Julius (16 oz)	220
Jamba Juice, Mango Mantra (16 oz)	170
Jamba Juice, Orange/Carrot (16 oz)	160
Jamba Juice, Passion Berry Breeze (16 oz)	150
Apple juice (8 oz)	116
Orange juice (8 oz)	112
Carrot juice (8 oz)	97
Campbell's V-8 (8 oz)	51

Not all fruit beverages are made from real juice. Some labeled "-ades," "fruit cocktails," or "fruit drinks" may offer as little as 5 percent juice. Just because something says it was made with juice doesn't mean it actually has much in it. Make sure the label reads "Made with 100 percent juice." If it doesn't, you're getting a drink made primarily from sugar water, colors, flavors, and a vitamin or two. Some labels are very deceptive. You see "100 percent" and think it means juice, when it may actually refer to some other ingredient. Kraft's orange drink Tang advertises that it offers 100 percent vitamin C, but it doesn't have any real juice in it. This means all the vitamin C you're getting is from added vitamins, not from real juice. Yes, you're still getting the vitamin, but you're not getting any of the other benefits offered by real fruit juice, and you're also getting artificial flavors and colors. And if you see the word "light" or "lite" on the label, you're expecting the product to have fewer calories, and it usually does – but the way they make it "light" is by adding water and charging you more. You can dilute your *real* fruit juice with water or sparkling water at home. This way you have a "light" drink for less money – along with all the wonderful benefits of eating (or drinking) a real food (as opposed to an artificial one).

One caution about drinking juice: Just because one glass is good, doesn't mean four are better. If the regular is good, super-sized is not better. A 32-ounce Jamba All Fruit Strawberry Whirl contains a whopping 77 grams of sugar. That's nineteen teaspoons, or more than a third of a cup of sugar. Another example of how fruit sugars can add up is found in the popular drink Snapple. Many flavors are made with 100 percent juice, but the juice comes from the condensed form; therefore, the sugars are concentrated. Snapple Fruit Punch (11.5-ounce size) has 170 calories and 40 grams of sugar, more than a Coke. Remember that fruit is sweet, even if it's natural, and it therefore contains a fair amount of sugar. So you want to keep the amount of fruit juice you drink to a minimum. The recommendation is that teens have no more than twelve ounces of juice a day.

I have to say something about Jamba Juice. I love the fact that the company promotes wonderful concoctions of fruits and vegetables with no additives, no artificial flavors, and no preservatives. I just wish they would also offer smaller sizes and flavors with less sugar.

MILK

Milk can be a replacement for one of your sodas during the day. If you choose low-fat or nonfat milk in place of a soda, your calorie and sugar intake will be cut way down. Milk is a good source of protein, calcium, and many important nutrients. It's great on cereal and even better with cookies. I mentioned earlier that having a protein with sugar helps keep the sugar from getting into your blood too quickly so you won't feel the sudden drop in blood sugar. Since the fat in all dairy products is

saturated and not the best for us, keep the fat content as low as you can tolerate. Not everyone likes the taste of nonfat (skim) milk, but 1 percent milk is usually well-received.

Milk

TYPE	CALORIES	FAT GRAMS
Chocolate milk, whole (8 oz)	208	8.5
Milk, whole (3.5% fat, 8 oz)	150	8.0
Milk, low-fat (2% fat, 8 oz)	121	4.7
Milk, low-fat (1% fat, 8 oz)	102	2.6
Milk, nonfat (8 oz)	86	0.4

If milk gives you an upset stomach, you may want to try the lactose-free version, acidophilus milk, or try soy or rice milk. I like low-fat vanilla soy milk on my cereal. It's sweet enough that I don't have to dip into the sugar bowl.

ALCOHOL

Beer, wine, and cocktails add calories in a big way – nearly double the calories one gets from protein and carbohydrates. A can of beer has about 156 calories in it, a glass of wine about 90, and normal-sized cocktails about 150–190. There are many reasons why alcohol is not encouraged when you're trying to lose weight. All kinds of alcohol appear to be very efficient in helping the body store fat. Alcohol is associated with an increased risk of stomach fat (a.k.a. "beer belly"), which is the worst kind of fat to carry in terms of your health. In addition, alcohol lowers inhibitions and can totally destroy your ability to make wise choices, dietary and otherwise. And you know that if you DO make a decision to drink, you need to find someone else to drive.

WATER

Water is the all-around best drink I can recommend. Most people don't know it but water itself is a nutrient, one that is vital to life and the operation of all your bodily functions. It is necessary for the digestion and metabolism of food. It hydrates your body, adding moisture to your organs and skin. It cleans out your digestive system and is very instrumental in keeping your bowels regular. If you're constipated, drink up. If you're bloated from eating too much sugar or salt, drink more water and you will feel lighter. If you feel tired, you may, in fact, be dehydrated; if so, drinking water will restore your energy. If you feel hungry, drink water before eating something. You may just be thirsty, and a glass of water may help decrease your appetite.

Most people don't drink enough water. How about you? How many glasses do you drink in a day? The standard recommendation is to drink about eight 8-ounce glasses per day. Do you come close? Try replacing some of your coffees or sodas with fresh water. Always have water close by to reduce hunger pangs and just to keep you from becoming dehydrated. You can bottle your own water at home and, for a little zip, add lemon, lime, a splash of apple juice, orange juice, cucumbers, or whatever flavor you like. Experiment and come up with a new drink.

Water is critical to all life. We can live without food for months, but we cannot go more than a few days without water. Normally I would recommend that you drink all the water you can, but a disturbing incident occurred recently that showed how anything can be taken to the extreme, even drinking water. A twenty-eight-year old woman recently died from water intoxication – that is, from drinking too much water. It was a stunt that she participated in to see how much water a person could drink without going to the bathroom. Apparently she consumed about two gallons and died later that day. Drinking excessive amounts of water throws off the body's balance of electrolytes, causing brain swelling, which leads to seizures, coma, and death. It demonstrates again how overindulging in anything is not just unhealthy – it can be deadly.

Putting It All Together

Does all of what you've read so far seem overwhelming to you? I hope that you now at least have some ideas about where you can cut down on calories, fat, and sugar in your diet and substitute less fattening and, hopefully, more healthy foods. Before I wrap things up, I have a few remaining thoughts I hope will help to guide you along the way.

Eating in Restaurants

Going out to eat with your parents or friends can be a nightmare when you are watching your calories. There are so many unknowns, so many choices. You don't want to avoid restaurants, so let me give you some tips that will help you stay on your program and continue to lose weight. At the start of the book I promised that you could do this diet and still have fun. So here are my guidelines for eating out.

1. *Cooking methods count.* Avoid words like *fried, breaded, coated,* and *creamy.* Order baked, grilled, roasted, or poached chicken, meats, or fish.

2. *Control condiments.* Ask for salad dressings, sauces, and condiments (butter, mayo) on the side. Sometimes you need only a taste. One great strategy for limiting the amount of salad dressing you eat is to order the dressing on the side, and then to dip

the very tip of your fork into the dressing before spearing a bite of salad. With this method, you'll notice that you eat only about a third of the dressing put before you, yet you still get a taste with every bite.

3. *Share meals.* Order a green salad, and share an entrée with a friend.

4. *Remove extra food.* Have the server take away the breadbasket and breadsticks immediately.

5. *Take home extra food.* When the server first sets your meal down, cut your entrée in half, and immediately ask for one of those halves to be boxed up as leftovers. Enjoy it for breakfast, lunch, or a snack the next day.

6. *Try an appetizer for your entrée.* However, make sure it's not deep-fried.

7. *Share dessert.* Order a single dessert for the entire table (unless there are, like, twelve people, in which case you should get two or three).

The following chart gets more specific. It lists many foods and ways of preparing them that you would typically order in American, Mexican, Italian, and Chinese restaurants. In the left-hand column are foods that are higher in fat and calories and therefore should be avoided (unless it's a special occasion). In the right-hand column are healthier, lower-calorie alternatives.

Restaurant Food Guide

USUALLY NOT OKAY	USUALLY OKAY
American Side Dishes	
Batter-fried shrimp	Shrimp cocktail
Dips	On the side
French-fried zucchini	Fruit

(cont'd.)

Restaurant Food Guide (cont'd.)

USUALLY NOT OKAY	USUALLY OKAY
French fries	Tomatoes
Cream soups	Broth or vegetable soup
Cobb salad	½ portion, no bacon
Regular dressing	Low-calorie dressing
Vegetable in cream sauce	Vegetable, no sauce
Buttered toast	Dry toast, jam on side
Potato/pasta salad	Fruit
Entrées	
Fried	Roasted
Deep fried	Broiled
Baked in gravy or sauce	Baked without sauce
Cooked in butter sauce	Poached
Breaded	Barbecued
Sausage, prime rib	Lean meats (or remove visible fat)
Chicken with skin	Remove skin
Sandwich on croissant	Sandwich on wheat bread
Hamburger	Grilled teriyaki
Potatoes	
Baked with butter	Sour cream, salsa, chili

(cont'd.)

Restaurant Food Guide (cont'd.)

USUALLY NOT OKAY	USUALLY OKAY
Fried skins	New potatoes
French- or home-fried	Steamed
Desserts	
Pastry	Fresh fruit
Cake	Angel food cake
Pudding	Custard
Ice cream	Sorbet
Pies, chocolate cakes, cheesecake	Split a piece with someone
Condiments	
Salad dressing or mayonnaise	Lite version
Tartar sauce	Ketchup
Cheese sauce	Mustard
Croutons	Steak sauce
Mexican	
Chips	Plain tortillas
Guacamole, sour cream, dressing	Salsa
Nachos	Bean burrito
Grande burrito	Chicken fajita
Chorizo sausage	Spicy beef, chicken
Covered in cheese	Salsa verde

(cont'd.)

Restaurant Food Guide (cont'd.)

USUALLY NOT OKAY	USUALLY OKAY
Covered in sour cream	With picante sauce
Molé sauce	Enchilada sauce
Salad in fried taco shell	Leave the shell
Crispy	Grilled
Italian	
Creamy white sauce (Alfredo)	Tomato sauce (marinara)
Stuffed with cheese	Stuffed with vegetables
White clam sauce	Red clam sauce
Pesto sauce	Marinara sauce
Saltimbocca	Cacciatore
Pancetta	Piccata
Breaded veal cutlets	Baked veal
Pepperoni pizza	Canadian bacon pizza
Chinese	
Egg rolls	Wonton soup
Barbecued ribs	Chicken wrapped in foil
Dumplings, fried	Dumplings, steamed
Sweet and sour sauce	Brown sauce
Breaded and fried	Hot and spicy sauce

(cont'd.)

Restaurant Food Guide (cont'd.)

USUALLY NOT OKAY	USUALLY OKAY
Crispy	Braised
Fried rice	Steamed white rice
Fried apples	Fortune cookie

Tips for Success

You have all the information you need to make your plan a success. Here are my final reminders:

- ✗ Make a plan for changing your behavior. Focus on what you can do, not on how much you want to lose.

- ✗ Start slowly. Most people want to lose ten pounds in the first week. This is not realistic or even possible. Permanent weight loss takes time. Aim to lose one or two pounds a week.

- ✗ Change one habit at a time. Even if you are eager to turn your world upside-down, forget it! Work on one meal or one snack only. When you feel comfortable with that, go on to another.

- ✗ At night, write down your next day's strategy. Be prepared for vulnerable times, and decide how you are going to handle these situations.

- ✗ Don't skip meals. It lowers your metabolism.

- ✗ Eat regularly. Don't go longer than five hours without eating. You will lose more weight this way even if you take in slightly more calories.

- ✗ Eat balanced meals, including protein, complex carbohydrates, and healthy fats.

- ✗ Honor your body by feeding it a variety of healthy foods.

✗ Say no to super-sized foods and drinks. You don't have to clean your plate when it's filled with too much food.

✗ Drink six to eight glasses of water a day. Water hydrates your cells, prevents hunger pangs, and helps you to keep your energy level up.

✗ Losing weight with a friend or group of supportive people helps because you can share your difficult times and successes with each other.

✗ Pay attention to what you're eating and how good it smells and tastes. Don't be distracted by the TV or a book.

✗ Eat slowly. It takes twenty minutes for your stomach to tell your brain you are full.

✗ Have a snack one hour before eating. A small snack helps some people to curb their appetite. (But if this strategy doesn't work for you, forget it.)

✗ Keep problem foods out of the house, and stock up on lower-calorie snacks. You are more likely to resist temptation if unhealthy and high-fat foods are not around.

✗ If you don't like something, don't eat it.

✗ Work on cutting out foods that have no nutritional value.

✗ If you really crave it, give in.

✗ Write down everything you eat, and roughly figure out the caloric and fat gram value. Do this for at least a few weeks, which should be long enough to grasp what you need to do to positively change your eating habits.

✗ When you give in to high-fat foods, forgive yourself and do better the next day. Don't starve or cut out a meal to catch up. Weight loss is a process, and you don't have to learn it perfectly in a few days or weeks.

✗ Start moving more, adding steps to your daily routine.

✗ Find an activity that you like and do it regularly.

✗ Don't let your weight keep you from activities or sports you enjoy.

✗ Keep reminding yourself of all the great things about you.

✗ Hang out with friends who support you and like you just the way you are.

✗ Concentrate on things other than your body. How can you make the world a better place?

✗ Keep picturing yourself as the person you know you can be.

You Can Do It!

Now you have all the tools you need to design your own safe diet plan. Believe it is possible and know that you are going to succeed. Losing weight won't change who you are. You are wonderful and fantastic right now. However, losing weight will likely help you feel better about yourself because you will feel healthier and more energetic. Congratulate yourself. You are on the path to making positive changes in one area of your life. And it's only the beginning. Who knows what you will decide to do next!

Resources

Internet Sites for Teens

HEALTH AND NUTRITION

www.smart-mouth.org
Interactive website providing nutrition information, recipes, articles, and games. Sponsored by the Center for Science in the Public Interest (CSPI).

www.caprojectlean.org
California Project LEAN's Food on the Run program, which promotes healthy eating and physical activity.

www.4girls.gov
4 Girls Health, sponsored by the National Woman's Health Information Center, offers information on nutrition, fitness, reading food labels, and a range of other topics, like safety, bullying, drugs, alcohol, and smoking.

www.girlpower.gov
Seeks to reinforce positive values among girls ages nine to thirteen. Sponsored by the U.S. Department of Health and Human Services.

www.FoodFacts.info
Database of twenty-seven fast-food restaurants and 2,600 menu items.

www.nutritiondata.com
Provides complete nutrient analysis of any food or recipe, from fruits to fast food.

SELF-ESTEEM

www.campaignforrealbeauty.com
Dove's Campaign for Real Beauty. See a video demonstrating how advertisers touch up average women to make them look like glamorous models.

www.teenshealth.org
Website for girls and guys dealing with how to improve your self-esteem and body image. Also provides info about food, fitness, emotional issues, and growing up. Includes discussions on fitness, safety, school, health, disease, sex, drugs, and alcohol.

www.girlsinc.org
A nonprofit organization that inspires all girls to be strong, smart, and bold.

www.freespirit.com
Click on "Teens." Free Spirit is a site that helps kids help themselves.

www.mindonthemedia.org
Mind on the Media promotes a healthy body image and expands the definition of what makes people beautiful.

www.newmoon.org
New Moon is a magazine for girls who want their voices to be heard and their dreams taken seriously.

www.bodypositive.com
Encourages boosting body image at any weight and any age and taking action to change media advertising.

GENERAL

www.bam.gov
Body and Mind, created by the Centers for Disease Control and Prevention, is beautifully designed to look like a comic. It helps teens learn

about their body, health, food, diseases, and physical activity. Games and quizzes make it a fun, interactive place to visit.

www.blubberbusters.com
A website for overweight kids or teens and their parents. Includes tips from other teens.

FOR PARENTS

www.epi.umn.edu/research/eat
Project EAT: Eating among Teens is a study designed to investigate the eating habits of adolescents. The study was created by investigators from the faculty of the University of Minnesota, Division of Epidemiology.

EATING DISORDERS

www.healthfinder.gov/justforyou
The U.S. Department of Health and Human Services sponsors this site, Health Finder for Teenagers.

www.geneenroth.com
The website of author Geneen Roth. Focuses on breaking free of emotional eating and the spiritual issues surrounding emotional eating. Includes offers for books, videos, workshops, and retreats.

www.something-fishy.org
Dedicated to raising awareness of eating disorders and providing support for individuals with eating disorders.

www.nationaleatingdisorders.org
National Eating Disorders Association provides information and programs on eating disorders.

www.raderprograms.com
The Rader Program treats a variety of eating disorders, including anorexia, bulimia, compulsive overeating, and night eating syndrome.

Weight-Loss Programs and Camps for Teens

www.shapedown.com
Shapedown is an all-inclusive program for kids, teens, and their par-

ents that was developed by faculty of the University of California at San Francisco School of Medicine.

www.campshane.com
Camp Shane is the original co-ed weight-loss camp. They advertise that it's not a fat camp.

www.camplajolla.com
Camp La Jolla is a customized weight-loss camp and fitness program for children, teens, and adults.

Books for Parents

Berg, Frances M., *Underage and Overweight: Our Childhood Obesity Crisis – What Every Family Needs to Know.* New York: Hatherleigh Press, 2005.

Deumark-Sztainer, Dianne, *I'm, Like, SO Fat! Helping Your Teen Make Healthy Choices about Eating and Exercise in a Weight-Obsessed World.* New York: The Guilford Press, 2005.

Ponton, Lynn E., M.D., *The Romance of Risk: Why Teenagers Do the Things They Do.* New York: Basic Books, 1997.

A Note to Parents

How You Can Help
Your Teen Lose Weight

The latest statistics indicate that kids today are fatter than they have ever been before. Some 17 percent of American children and teens are obese, and millions more are overweight. It's time to talk about it. It's time to take action. Obesity puts children, as it does adults, at greater risk for high blood pressure, heart disease, diabetes, respiratory illnesses, orthopedic disorders, as well as psychological and social problems.

What's a parent to do? While the situation is indeed serious and needs attention, DO NOT PANIC and sign your child up for an expensive program or buy the latest diet book. Fast weight loss is more harmful than healthful, and if the child can't comply, the feelings of failure are psychologically damaging to their sense of self-worth. Research shows that losing weight permanently comes from a slow retraining process that involves a change in attitude toward food, eating less, and moving the body more. *Safe Dieting for Teens* not only covers these facets of weight loss, it also integrates each component into the teen's lifestyle. The program is effective because it allows teens to decide, from all the possibilities listed, what changes work best for them. It works because they are taking responsibility for their weight loss. *They* are in control, not you.

This is your teen's program. Still, you can help from the sidelines.

1. **Read the book to understand the program.** You should be informed about what they are doing. You should feel comfortable knowing that this book presents a safe and reasonable way to lose weight and not some hyped-up scheme. I recommend that you read the book *before* they do (or obtain your own copy) because I'm asking them to write in it, and then it becomes their personal journal.

2. **Do not insist that your teen diet if he or she is not ready.** Losing weight has to be self-motivated. My goal is to motivate teens by showing how doable the program is. Nagging is not productive. It will hurt their self-image and self-esteem, and will also encourage resentment toward you. Let them know you love them no matter what they weigh.

3. **Do not assume responsibility for their problem.** If they show interest in dieting, proceed carefully. Don't take control and sign them up for the program that worked for you; don't put them on your diet. Let them find their own way. Unless you're asked, hold your tongue.

4. **Don't be overly concerned with instant results.** This plan teaches food exchanges and new behavior patterns. Change is difficult for anyone. No matter how anxious your teen is to lose weight, she or he will not always make the best choices. *Allow them to practice their plan at their own pace.*

5. **Encourage physical activity.** Help your child(ren) find ways of adding steps to their daily routine. You can park farther away from the store. Ask them to wash the car, vacuum the carpet, or walk the dog. If they want to sign up for dancing or tennis, be supportive.

6. **Limit TV and video time.** Studies show that television contributes to weight gain. It monopolizes time that could be spent on more active endeavors and is associated with increased snacking. Furthermore, the body's metabolic rate drops between 12 percent and 16 percent while watching the tube. According to

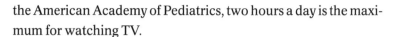

the American Academy of Pediatrics, two hours a day is the maximum for watching TV.

7. **Ask your teen how you can best help.** Teens need your support. What foods do they want in the house? You could talk about foods they like that are healthier and lower in calories. You don't have to restructure everything your family has done for years or give up family traditions, but working together on their program could be a fun family project. On the other hand, if they ask you not to be so helpful, back off.

8. **Spend time alone with your teen.** Talk about all the various things that are going on in their lives, like school, friends, music, or fashion. Let them know you are interested in who they are and that you love and appreciate their unique qualities. Praise is always worthwhile. If your teen (probably daughter) is into it, take her to a health spa and spend time talking about the foods they offered and classes she enjoyed. But do this only if she is interested.

9. **Be a role model.** Are you overweight? Do you want to lose weight too? This book can also help you. But don't use your teen's copy, since it is their own personal program. Buy your own to write in, and record your own behaviors and goals. Also bear in mind that while the thought of "dieting" together may sound good to you, it may not be how your teen wants to bond. So be open to their feelings and proceed with caution.

10. **Be patient.** Kids love to test parents. One day they want you to buy fruit for snacking and the next day they may criticize you for not having any goodies in the house. Losing weight is not an easy process. Be helpful, but avoid the guilt trap. Ultimately, it's their process. They will feel great when they have done it themselves.

This guide is part of *Safe Dieting for Teens*. It is meant to be used in conjunction with the book and is designed to assist parents and others working in a helping capacity with teens who are using the book. It is not meant as a therapy guide or as an individual program for any other purpose.

Index

A
addiction, amphetamine, 34
aerobic exercise, 67, 71, 72–74
alcohol, 137–138
American Journal of Clinical Nutrition, 130
amino acids, 93–94
amphetamines, 34
anemia, 41
anorexia nervosa, 2, 39–41
anxiety, 69
appetite control, 69
appetite suppressants, 34–35
arthritis, 15
aspartame, 132
Atkins diet, 29–30
Atkins, Robert, 29
Au Bon Pain, 108, 109

B
Baja Fresh, 109–110
balance of food groups, 93, 145
Banquet Frozen Dinners, 115
bars, food, 123
beauty, unrealistic standard of, 8, 38, 50–52
bee pollen, 36
behavioral changes, 80
Better Homes and Gardens, 33
"better than" food plan, 48
beverages, 127–139; alcohol, 137–138; diet sodas, 131–132; energy drinks, 132–133; fruit juice, 134–136; milk, 136–137; sodas, 129–131; sports drinks, 133–134; Starbucks, 128–129; water, 138–139, 146
bingeing, 21, 26–27, 41–43
birth control pills and weight gain, 22
blood pressure, high, 15, 41
blood sugar, 21, 94

body style, full-figured, 19–20
body temperature, low, 41
bone development, retarded, 15
Boston Market, 116–117
breakfast, 90, 100–106; balancing food groups, 101; breakfast bars, 97, 120; healthy suggestions for, 102–106; skipping, 101
Bryant, Kobe, 49
bulimia nervosa, 41–43
Burger King, 90, 112
butter, 14, 90, 102

C
caffeine, 35, 36, 132–133
cakes, 125–126
calorie information, 86, 88–89
calories: burning, 67, 76–78, 82; ideas for cutting, 91; listed on food label, 97; recommended, 26–27
campaignforrealbeauty.com, 7–8
candy, 124–125
carbohydrates: inability to process, 22–23; recommended, 94–95; refined versus complex, 31; sugars, 97–99
carbonated beverages, 129–131
cardio exercise, 71, 72–74
Carl's Jr., 107–108
Carpenter, Karen, 38
cereal, 90, 97, 98, 102
chart, food, 86
Cheerios, 97, 98
cheese, 106–107
childbearing, 19
chips, 124
cholesterol, high, 15
Cinnabon, 102
cold, intolerance to, 41
communication, importance of, 17–18
complex carbohydrates, 31, 94–95

Food Record and Calorie Log

Week #: _____   From: _____   To: _____

Write down the foods you eat under each meal heading. Record the calories under Calories "In." Write your exercise for the day, and record the calories it burns under Calories "Out." By subtracting Calories "Out" from Calories "In" you get your net calorie intake for the day.

MONDAY	Calories "In"	TUESDAY	Calories "In"	WEDNESDAY	Calories "In"	THURSDAY	Calories "In"	FRIDAY	Calories "In"	SATURDAY	Calories "In"	SUNDAY	Calories "In"
Breakfast		Breakfast		Breakfast		Breakfast		Breakfast		Breakfast		Breakfast	
Snack		Snack		Snack		Snack		Snack		Snack		Snack	
Lunch		Lunch		Lunch		Lunch		Lunch		Lunch		Lunch	
Snack		Snack		Snack		Snack		Snack		Snack		Snack	
Dinner		Dinner		Dinner		Dinner		Dinner		Dinner		Dinner	
Snack		Snack		Snack		Snack		Snack		Snack		Snack	
Total Calories "In" (A)		Total Calories "In" (A)		Total Calories "In" (A)		Total Calories "In" (A)		Total Calories "In" (A)		Total Calories "In" (A)		Total Calories "In" (A)	
EXERCISE	Calories "Out" (B)	EXERCISE	Calories "Out" (B)	EXERCISE	Calories "Out" (B)	EXERCISE	Calories "Out" (B)	EXERCISE	Calories "Out" (B)	EXERCISE	Calories "Out" (B)	EXERCISE	Calories "Out" (B)
Net Calories (A-B)		Net Calories (A-B)		Net Calories (A-B)		Net Calories (A-B)		Net Calories (A-B)		Net Calories (A-B)		Net Calories (A-B)		Net Calories (A-B)	

Goals for next week:

Total Calories for the Week: _____